P.O.W.E.R. TOOLS @ WORK

Helping Leaders

Build a Strong, Engaged & Connected Culture

Published by Bock's Office Publishing
Fargo, North Dakota

Bock, Jodee A. with Levos, Brenda J. P.

P.O.W.E.R. Tools At Work: Helping Leaders Build a Strong, Engaged & Connected Culture

ISBN 978-0-9785722-5-9

Printed in the U.S.A.

Praise for P.O.W.E.R. Tools @ Work

"Jodee Bock has been sharing these P.O.W.E.R. Tools with our teams for several months, and we are definitely seeing results as we work to shift our culture. The ideas and resources will challenge you to seek opportunities and inspire possibilities within yourself that will inspire achievement in work and personal life events. The resources and tools within the book assist in accomplishing tasks and creating a culture of cohesiveness, understanding, and success."

- Stacie Garland, RN- Nursing Manager
  CHI Lisbon Area Health Services

"Guiding the contribution of brilliance of others requires us as leaders to relate with them at levels beyond the day-to-day, beyond the mundane with which we have become comfortable, beyond the data and the performance ratios. P.O.W.E.R. Tools @ Work provides practical ideas for breaking important conversations down into manageable and applicable pieces that can immediately be put into practice."

- Lance Secretan, former CEO of a Fortune 100
  company, university professor, award-winning
  columnist, poet, author,
  and outdoor athlete

"P.O.W.E.R. Tools @ Work provides sensible, effective, and applicable ideas for inspiring and motivating leaders and teams. It's a great resource for anyone who is ready to take personal accountability for effectively navigating and leading in business and in life."

– Steve Farber, President of Extreme Leadership, Inc. and the author of four books including *Love is Just Damn Good Business*

"P.O.W.E.R. Tools @ Work is the ultimate guidebook for leaders of all shapes and sizes, offering insights into how to claim and reclaim our power for change in the world. Packed with actionable insights that hit you right between the eyes, and encouraging you to do something differently, P.O.W.E.R. Tools will help you lead the intentional life you've always hoped of living, but didn't know how - until now."

- Phil Gerbyshak, sales trainer, sales speaker and podcaster

CONTENTS

Like tools,
ideas
are only effective
**when
they are
utilized**

AUTHOR'S PREFACE

Everybody who has ever taken a shower has had a good idea.

But not everybody dries off and puts together a plan for taking that idea from concept to reality. This project is the result of not only a good idea, but a collaboration that allowed the best of both of us to come together, in a MasterMind setting, to bring it to life.

Like the birth of any concept, it wasn't without its share of pain and angst. Deadlines can be joy killers, but there is nothing like the feeling of accomplishment that comes as the result of pushing through the tough times.

We've been having conversations about awareness, spirituality, effectiveness, business, creativity, leadership, and possibility for years. We've studied *Think and Grow Rich* many, many times, and have read and studied – and, in our own separate journeys – applied many of the concepts we will share with you.

While Jodee is the main author and most of the stories are hers, this project would never have come to be if Brenda hadn't suggested it. It takes guts and grace to drive a project such as this one, and it was a true collaboration to bring it from concept to reality.

We know that you will find at least one new idea in each chapter of the book. It may be a brand new idea, or it may be reinforcement of an idea you've been kicking around for a while on your own. In any case, we know that, like tools, ideas are only effective when they are utilized.

We are committed to providing ideas and suggestions to get you and your organization to see things from a different perspective, and actually do something with your awareness. When the why is big enough, the how tends to show up: for your organization as it has with us as we created *P.O.W.E.R. Tools @ Work*. Enjoy!

Jodee & Brenda

We are confident you will find value in P.O.W.E.R. Tools @ Work

If your ORGANIZATIONAL DESTINATION is:

- More effective **COMMUNICATION**
- Improved **PRODUCTIVITY**
- Organizational **HEALTH**
- Employee **ENGAGEMENT**
- Enhanced **CORPORATE RESPONSIBILITY**

If your INDIVIDUAL DESTINATION is:

- Clarity of **IMPACT**
- Building **AUTHENTIC RELATIONSHIPS**
- Unleashing **CREATIVITY**
- Owning your **GREATNESS**
- Shedding the **SHOULDS**

Nothing
changes
until
something
changes

and guess what?
You're
going to
go first.

INTRODUCTION

If you're being honest, your life is pretty darn good.

You have within you the capacity to achieve goals and meet expectations. You've survived every challenge you've met up to this point in your life.

If you are reading this, you have the wherewithal and the knowledge to read, and that's more than 17% of the human population can say.[1]

Yet, if you are like nearly every other human being on the planet – and we're pretty sure you are – there is something in your work and/or your personal life that you wish could be different.

Not necessarily better, but definitely different.

You may know exactly what that is, or you may have no clue. Or maybe you're somewhere in between. It can feel like a nagging sensation or sound like a clanging alarm.

You may be, like Thomas Edison recognized, "restless and discontent," which he noted was a

necessity for progress. Or you may be, like Albert Einstein noted, "passionately curious." Or you may just be doing a favor to a friend or colleague who suggested you take a look at this concept.

Something inside you realizes that if you keep doing the same thing over and over – or resist doing something new – you will be destined to remain stuck.

You ***NEED*** something to change, or you merely ***WISH*** something would.

If you knew exactly what that was, you would have addressed it by now, before you got to this frantic and frenzied and stressed place.

Yet most of the time, when you're the most frustrated and upset, you are wishing and hoping and praying that ***THEY*** will do something – ANYTHING – to make things better.

Or maybe you're just starting to recognize and be irritated by something: something ***THEY*** are doing or being or saying … or they aren't.

And ***THEY*** keep following you around.

If only ***THEY*** would DO something!

Maybe it's time to let you in on a little secret: This book isn't for ***THEM***. It's for ***YOU***.

Nothing changes until something changes and guess what? You're going to go first.

Many humans are in search of achievement. They know there is something out there they want, but they don't know exactly how to get it.

Or they are really clear how to get it, they just want to get there faster. Or they are wandering aimlessly but don't even realize it. All are great reasons to understand the distinction between

hustling and grinding and making and forcing and motivating

and

allowing and aligning and creating and seeking opportunity and inspiring possibility.

Throughout this book we're going to make a case for choosing your personal ***POWER*** in order to achieve, attract, experience and become anything you've ever desired for yourself and your life, both at work and outside of work.

Bold claim? Perhaps. Yet generations of humans have understood the possibilities that exist inside of each of us but remain untapped in our external pursuits. You don't *NEED* anything you don't already have: you may just not realize that right now. It's our quest to provide **information** – in the form of this book and the learning opportunities around it – and also **inspiration** – in the spirit we are confident will grab hold of you if you are ready to tap into it.

You have been gifted with an intellect, a mind, a body, a place in the human race. No matter what it isn't, there are a myriad of things it is. And, whether

When you are **inspired**, you can't not **BE** inspiring.

Your **energy** is magnetic.

you acknowledge or remember that or not, it's still true. If you're like many – maybe even most – humans, you take those things that were gifted to you free at birth for granted.

The ideas in this book are just that: ideas. They are not demands or dogmas or systems or processes or guarantees. They are ideas to get you thinking about things just a little bit differently.

Henry Ford, industrialist and brilliant inventor, said that "Thinking is the hardest work there is, which is probably the reason so few engage in it."

Well, no one ever said it was going to be easy. But it really is very simple. Instead of trying to force things to happen and make things happen and demand things either change or stay the same, we're going to invite you to consider that *force* comes from outside of you. ***Forcing*** something to change (or to stop changing), along with ***making*** something happen and ***demanding*** something of yourself or others automatically creates resistance. That's what force does.

Forcing is like ***motivation*** – it's external and based on fear. It comes from the personality, the senses.

Power, on the other hand, is like ***inspiration***. It can be recognized and experienced only through inner awareness. It's not even a *doing*: it's a being. When you are inspired, you can't not ***BE*** inspiring. Your energy is magnetic. You do things from a place of authenticity and a desire to be connected. Where motivation is based on someone else's motive (usually fear, remember?), inspiration is based on an internal knowing - something much more like love.

I have experienced the difference between force and inspiration first-hand.

Growing up, my family owned a small café and ice cream store where I worked as a waitress and cashier from the time I was 12 until I was 18. It wasn't the most difficult job in the world, but as a youngster, it wasn't exactly the way I would have chosen to spend my free time.

That must be where I first determined that a job must be something you don't love so you can make money to do the things you do love. After all, it's a job - it's "work."

So when it came time for me to choose a college major, I determined that computer science would fit that bill. Hard work, but good money. As you can probably imagine, that freshman year was a bit challenging for someone who preferred writing and communication to formulas and statistics.

On top of working desperately to figure out the foreign concepts that math was presenting to me, I was dealing with the challenges of being the only freshman on the varsity basketball team. As a person who derived her worth from external sources like fickle fans or discerning professors, you can imagine the angst I went through when I got my first C in Calculus I, and was put on the junior varsity team to "get more playing time."

That second semester when my class list included Calculus II, and the pull was especially strong to focus more on the court than in the computer lab, I decided that something needed to change. I made the decision to drop Calc II and pick up a journalism class, which allowed me more head space for basketball. I moved up to becoming the sixth player, and scored 10 points in the national championship game later that winter.

Switching my major to communication and English writing as a sophomore, I began to see that, at least in college courses, it was possible to enjoy the work. I started to wonder though: how would that translate to actual employment?

It took me a while to find my stride. A long while. A really, long while. In fact, it involved a series of career shifts that had me moving away from what I didn't like in pursuit of something I did. Until that last job, where my boss didn't appreciate that I was working on a project for *his* boss. He confronted me, asking me point blank: "who do you work for: her or me?" In order to keep the project, I had to agree to report my daily schedule to him in 15-minute increments.

Not too inspiring. And over time, I started losing my steam for that very same project that had first excited me. It was just too exhausting to feel that I had to look over my shoulder in case he caught me doing something that I hadn't reported on my time sheet.

It began to feel like a full-time job for him to keep his finger on me, and a full-time job for me to keep trying desperately to fit into his insecurity.

The straw that finally broke that poor, tired camel's back was when that boss, who had hired me to work on what was called People Systems Development, for which it was, by nature, difficult to measure results, told me that what I did was "touchy-feely crap that makes me puke." If that wasn't enough, he also told me, in response to my desire to build relationships with potential clients, "business has nothing to do with relationships."

How did I get here? This experience reminded me of my freshman year of college: trying desperately to fit in to some random (and maybe even made up) authority figure's plan while being pulled in a seemingly opposite yet much more fulfilling direction.

The good news is that it was this job that provided me the impetus to finally start my own business. I left Corporate America as an employee so I could help people stay and make a difference. If the best workers end up being the ones who eventually leave as I felt I needed to, my fear was that we would be left with robots – literally or figuratively – to run our corporations and organizations. I had to believe my work experience didn't have to be everyone's experience, and that what I had gone through didn't have to be in vain.

I have loved discovering that there do exist those stories of positive work cultures where leaders

celebrate their employees' talents and gifts and allow them to shine. These leaders leverage their employees' skills for the benefit of the employees themselves, the organizational culture and, ultimately, the customer.

Among those companies I've had an opportunity to study is the online retail organization Zappos. If you ever have a chance to visit their headquarters in Las Vegas, you will experience firsthand a culture like very few others.

Core values are key at Zappos, and employees are encouraged to bring their true personalities to their cubicles. Tours are conducted regularly, and tour guides direct groups through the maze, guided by street signs. Giant license plates hang from the ceiling, noting employees' length of service. On the day I visited, I met Jerry, the mayor of Zappos, whose job seemed to include the duty of making sure my group felt welcomed and appreciated.

Our guide helped us find our way through a jungle with huge palm trees and overgrown plants in one section, and a department that was decorated like a pirate ship in another. They were holding some sort of potluck lunch that day, and were having more fun than is typically encouraged at work. We even walked right past CEO Tony Hsieh's cubicle, right in the middle of the chaos.

His entire career journey, including and prior to Zappos, is the impetus behind Hsieh's book *Delivering Happiness*, in which he gives several examples of how thinking long-term and following your passions first can lead to not just a profitable business, but a happy life for everyone - employees, leaders, and customers. As you focus on making people around you happy, you can't help but increase your own happiness.

You Lead You

This is a book for ***leaders***. Not necessarily people with a title, or position, or longevity, but people who are willing to step up and into their own personal power. People who are ready to invite a new outcome at work. People who realize that a little bit of curiosity and a little bit more courage will inevitably produce a different solution. Not the right answer, necessarily, but a new and different possibility.

When you are at the cause of this awareness and the consequential shift that happens as a result, you have a huge opportunity. If you only recognize the effects, you will be forced to wait for instruction or permission to take action, and then it will be as a result of someone else's direction instead of your own.

If you are not willing to tap into your power now, you will have to take your experience of life, whether at work or at home, from someone who uses force because he/she doesn't know better. That's been the way things have gotten done. Motivation has its own purpose, and often it's a louder and stronger and more forceful way than true purpose has been.

So, whether you have any of the external signs of success or not, you are always the leader of you. Always and in all ways.

Something inside of you is calling desperately to you to step up and live the life you were created to live. That something inside of you is your inner leader.

Now if you have a title or position inside a corporation or organization, you might begin to believe that that title automatically gives you some clout in the leadership department.

For all intents and purposes, it really should, shouldn't it?

But that's not always the case. Surely you know someone somewhere who's been bestowed with a title or position but shows none (or very few) of the characteristics we would use if describing the ideal leader. That's not you, of course, but we're sure you know some people like that.

Inside a corporate structure, you have a huge opportunity to influence a lot of people, whether you realize it or not. John Maxwell, leadership guru and author of many books about this topic, says that leadership is influence. Nothing more, nothing less. So, if you recognize and capitalize on your opportunity to do just that, you're a leader.

You will enjoy and learn something from this book if you are:

- Looking to get more engaged in something in your life.
- Realizing that the way you've been can only get you where you currently are: in order to get a different result, something has to shift.
- Beginning to connect the dots of your past and seeing that every time you have a challenge – or a victory – you are the common denominator.
- Tired of talking about what's wrong and ready to look deeper for what's possible.
- Curious and courageous enough to give a new idea a shot.

Surviving ... or Thriving?

We humans are not meant to be alone. We are social creatures, and we thrive when we find our tribe. Whether it's an online community, a support system, a MasterMind study group, or an in-person meet-up, most humans are happiest when they are accepted and celebrated and supported.

Living things react positively to those actions which are life-supportive, and they react negatively to those that are not: this is fundamental to our species' survival. Plants instinctively grow toward the sun as it provides life-giving nutrients and warmth. Humans are similar. We crave positive reinforcement and acceptance for

not only who we are, but who we are becoming, and as we grow, we follow that source.

But if you are only interested in surviving your life, you will never know what it's like to actually thrive. We don't have to think too much about merely surviving: our reptile brain – that part of our reactive system also known as the Fight or Flight response - will help us out in that regard. That reptile brain, the limbic system, is designed so that our species will survive danger.

But to live our best lives, mere survival is not enough.

In his book *Drive: The Surprising Truth About What Motivates Us*, Daniel Pink has pinned down some very intriguing aspects of human behavior. He says we either do the same thing over and over in a certain way – programmed and conditioned – or we feel compelled to come up with a new process every time we do something because there are no set instructions to follow. The first approach is left-brained or algorithmic, and the second is right-brained or heuristic.

This isn't news to us, right? We either want someone else to tell us what to do, or we reinvent our own ways.

Pink notes that external rewards work well for those who are algorithmic, but not so well for the heuristic folks.

His research shows that the secret to high performance isn't biological, or reward-and-punishment, but instead the deep-seated human desire to take charge of our own lives, to continue to learn and grow and expand, and to live a life of significance.

In 1943 Abraham Maslow created what has become a standard theory in human development: his Hierarchy of Needs. Pink's work parallels Maslow's in that they both agree that growth needs do not stem from a lack of something, but rather from a desire to grow as a person.

Every person is capable, and most have the desire, to move up the hierarchy toward a level of self-actualization. But if the lower level needs are not satisfied, progress toward the higher levels will be disrupted.

Humans really are searching for connection, and the way we have traditionally gotten that connection is through validation and appreciation. If the only way to receive that validation is externally, it will become a never-ending battle for worthiness and recognition, often at the expense of authenticity and what Napoleon Hill, in the business classic *Think and Grow Rich*, calls creative imagination.

If you are waiting for someone else to notice your amazing work, you never have to be accountable to yourself. Modeling the forceful way of motivating others then becomes the only way others learn, and personal power loses its charge.

Yet if we believe that everyone is motivated (outside) or inspired (inside) the same way, we will fail miserably as leaders. Neglecting to understand our employees' and associates' unique skills and talents as well as their learning styles leaves untold potential untapped.

Working to convince others instead of inspiring them will never produce the outcomes most leaders would say they want (if they are honest); yet that's what they end up doing because they think it's the shortest way to get to the desired outcome.

And that's if the leader has taken the time and effort and energy to plan a desired outcome.

Again, there is the external way to do that and the internal way.

We can't help you decide your desired outcome. That's completely up to you the business owner. Or you the entrepreneur. Or you the mom. Or you the entry-level employee.

Everyone has a core desire. They just might not know what it is. You have the ability to use your power for anything from a high-level corporate mission to a daily action plan. Just don't allow yourself to use the excuse "I don't know what I really want" anymore.

Just stop it. No more excuses.

Clarify your "want" and get started. Or just put this book back on the shelf because nothing can help you until you get clear that there is some want or some need that is nagging at you to allow it to be born.

Until you are at least committed to believing that there is something inside you - either personally or professionally - that you don't currently have, you are destined to remain stuck in a rut. And the only difference between a rut and a grave is the dimension.

P.O.W.E.R.

Purpose
Open Mindedness
Wisdom
Energy
Responsibility

Uncover those hidden and untapped sources inside that you may have neglected, forgotten about, or not yet discovered.

P.O.W.E.R. is an acronym we're using to uncover those hidden and untapped sources inside that you may have neglected, forgotten about, or not yet discovered.

The P.O.W.E.R. tools offered in this book will provide you an expanded perspective from which to see your place in the world. Instead of merely surviving, and fighting desperately to avoid change and evolution, you have the choice to be at the forefront of your own growth. When you remember that you always have choices, you will have a much better opportunity to really live every day of your life, not just stay upright until your time is over.

When you understand your own personal P.O.W.E.R., you will realize, as Dorothy did in the Wizard of Oz, that you've had everything you need inside of you all along. It's just a matter of turning it on.

Now are you ready to decide?

What are P.O.W.E.R. Tools?

Tools are resources. They are utilized to assist in accomplishing a task. Often tools are needed when fixing something that's broken, or when constructing something from scratch. Tools might also be utilized not just to fix or construct something physical, but also to assist in building or repairing something conceptually.

When you know what you desire, utilizing a power tool gets you there much more efficiently and effectively. Tapping into the power available to each of us will allow longer-term relationships to be built. Long-term relationships support the structure as well as infuse the heart and soul and spirit - the intangibles - into the culture of a community, a home, an organization or a corporation.

The title of the book, ***P.O.W.E.R. Tools @ Work***, implies that the tools can be utilized at your place of work, but also that they will only be effective when they are put to work. And since most people work not only at the place that pays a salary or a wage but also when moving any project from start to finish, it is our commitment that the tools in this book will be of major assistance in any situation, provided you know what it is you are constructing or repairing.

If you don't know better, you can't do better. Humans have spent a lot of time and effort and energy over millennia trying desperately to keep doing what isn't working so they can avoid having to learn that there might be a better way than the way they've always done it. They keep busy so they won't have to think. They know they need to fix things, and solve problems, and they spend most of their waking hours putting the hammer down to keep others in line.

The problem, however, is that if the only tool you have in your toolbox is a hammer, you will only ever be looking for nails. And if you can't find the nails, you will turn the screws and the staples and the fasteners into nails so you can be busy and tell yourself you're productive.

Most workers have that mentality. They want the freedom they envision for themselves at the place they work, but they don't seem to want the accountability it will require to get there.

When you ***force*** things to happen, or ***push*** people to do things, or ***rush*** through a project, you often get results that are much less favorable than if you had taken the proper time to plan for the construction. Grabbing a screwdriver and using the handle to pound in a nail might produce a desired result eventually, but it will probably also produce frustration and impatience.

POWER TO do something is freedom; ***POWER OVER*** someone or something is force.

This book and learning opportunity will focus primarily on power as it relates to personal, intrinsic power which comes from inspiration. Of course, there will be times force and motivation are needed. You wouldn't decide to create a dialogue with others if you see a fire in the corner of the room. You would force the safety issue.

These ***P.O.W.E.R. TOOLS*** are effective in building relationships, bonding teams together, and enhancing engagement and positive culture.

Ideas for Using These Tools

Each section of the book includes tools you can use to achieve a desired result. They will only be useful when you use them. If one tool or idea doesn't assist in the achievement of your desired result, there are others to try.

If nothing seems to work to get you where you desire to go, you may want to look for the common denominator. If you find that common denominator is you, good news! In that case you already have everything you need to achieve or experience or attract to you whatever you truly desire, because it's already inside of you.

Tap into the ***POWER*** and you won't need to force anything.

If you're even a little bit interested in learning, you will find value in this book. Either it will reinforce your current viewpoint or it will provide ideas to move you in a new direction. The key is to identify a couple of pain points and decide for yourself if you're ready to shift that pain from what isn't working to what is possible.

Pain is inevitable; suffering is optional. When you finally give up your need to be right, you will find relief from the pain of regret, and can move it to the pain of achievement and pushing through what you think is your comfort zone, but which I would argue is more like your familiar zone instead. After all, what's truly comfortable about the nagging pain of regret?

There are several ways to get the most out of this book and the ideas contained herein. All are suggestions – none are prescriptions. Discernment is a big part of personal development, so the ability to decide which works best to achieve a desired result is part of your own personal journey. One piece of advice, however: don't expect to get the ultimate results by doing this on your own.

Most people are either 1) their worst enemy or 2) a horrible accountability partner for themselves because they don't value themselves enough to step into a new level of greatness.

The information presented here may not be world-shatteringly new. You probably have heard some of this before, it may just be arranged and suggested in new ways. Regardless, what you ***know*** or even what you ***learn*** is never as important or as meaningful as what you choose to ***apply***. No matter how you study this material, what's truly important is that you *DO SOMETHING* with it. That's why this book will focus heavily on application.

The most important reminder is to have a desired outcome. If you want to read the book first just to get a feel for the information, OK. But it will be much more applicable if you first pick a destination or a project or a wish or, in the best case, a burning desire or an ideal outcome. Allow the tools to be your GPS, guiding you to that desired destination.

With that in mind, here are a few suggestions:

1. Read it with a group or team at work or in a community or family.
2. Pick one activity or exercise from the PURPOSE section to start on a Monday. Then move to OPEN-MINDEDNESS on Tuesday, WISDOM on Wednesday, ENERGY on Thursday, and RESPONSIBILITY on Friday.

Continue this rotation until you get through all the activities. This will take you through three months, or one quarter of a year. A 90-day time period is usually a good time to see measurable results.

3. Pick one section of the book and go through that one for one week at a time. Example: Pick PURPOSE for the first week and do one activity per day in that section. Then move on to OPEN-MINDEDNESS for week two, etc. This will take you through five weeks of material. Then start over Week Six with PURPOSE. This will give you a more thorough dip into each section.
4. Pick any activity that calls to you and find an accountability partner who will take this journey with you. Check in with each other regularly (daily is best) by phone or text. This doesn't have to be a long call (five minutes) but it needs to happen consistently.
5. Make up your own routine. Just be committed to your desired outcome.

As you are contemplating your own reasons for using these tools, keep in mind that a RESPONSE comes from thinking; a REACTION comes from not thinking.

This toolbox has RESPONSES, not REACTIONS. You've done very well without us in the reaction department. It's time now to THINK instead.

Team Tools

If using the tools with teams, it is highly recommended that you conduct some sort of personality assessment first, just so you know each other better and can tap into what makes the individuals in your organization tick.

There are some low- or no-cost tools available including, but not limited to, the **DISC Assessment,** which we find to be simple to understand and to explain. More than two million people have taken the 15-minute DISC assessment offered for free at Tony Robbins' website. This assessment helps to better understand personality type and behavior style. Developed by psychologist William Moulton Marston, the DISC assessment examines how an individual ranks in the four areas of behavior - Dominance, Influence, Steadiness, and Conscientiousness. It is designed for both individuals who want to identify and maximize their strengths and motivators, and organizations looking to integrate high-performance teams.[2]

You will find other assessment suggestions at our website: www.powertoolsatwork/toolbox.

In the area of **PURPOSE**, you will dig deeper into the WHY of actions, beliefs, behaviors, and even those deep-seated thoughts that limit your possibilities.

In the area of **OPEN-MINDEDNESS**, you will focus on Future Pacing, or acknowledging those old stories that might keep you from creating the future of your dreams.

WISDOM allows an exploration into the past, not to dwell there, but to learn from your experiences and your knowledge, and to take the lessons from those memories into your present actions.

In the **ENERGY** section you will work on putting language to the way things feel so you can alter your experience, if necessary, to produce those feelings you desire instead.

And in the **RESPONSIBILITY** section you will realize that whatever action you decide to take will produce a result, and the effects of those actions are up to you.

At the end of each section you will find a list of tools: ***Conversational Tools***, which give you an idea of what to say in certain situations, and ***Experiential Tools***, which you can use in a variety of ways either for yourself or for members of your team.

As you create more fulfilling and engaging workplaces, cultures, and experiences for people, it will be your responsibility as a leader, regardless of your title or your position, to help yourself and eventually others to take new action in order to produce new results.

When your routines become stuck, it is more difficult to recognize new patterns of possibility as you struggle just to keep your head above water. This is exactly the time you would benefit most from grabbing the life preserver and questioning everything.

Stubborn or recurrent problems are often symptoms of deeper issues. Quick fixes may seem convenient,

but they often solve only the surface issues and waste precious resources that could otherwise be used to tackle the real cause.

P.O.W.E.R. Tools @ Work allows any individual or team to tap into the unique abilities that might be looked at as commodities. But with the proper charge - the soul, the spirit, the ***POWER*** - any project can be infused with the talent and skills and gifts that give your organization the edge.

And that edge begins with you.

1 https://ourworldindata.org/literacy
2 https://www.tonyrobbins.com/disc/

Your clear vision is your driving force, it's the purpose behind the moves you make.

Part One: PURPOSE

Your Desired Outcome

[Synonyms - reason, impetus, objective, goal, WHY, vision]

You have a dream.

"Wouldn't it be great if __________," you think to yourself.

"I wish ____________"

"Someday maybe ______________"

All of these seemingly random thoughts are clues to your true desire, whether that's at work, at home, or just for you.

If you're like many people, your practical side takes over as soon as you allow yourself to think about a possibility. "If I don't know the ***HOW*** of it, what is the use?" your responsible side tells you.

That's exactly why it's so important to talk about the whole idea of ***PURPOSE***. So, let's go there.

You have to determine what you know and what you don't know when you endeavor to build something new. Just as you need a plan and a blueprint to build a house, you need that same vision to build a culture – or anything you want to take from your head to the real world. Anything that's not green or water or mountains or space was created twice: first in the mind of the creator and then in real life. So, having a clear vision is the first step.

Without a clear objective, activity turns into busyness. Purpose is multi-faceted. It can be as simple as picking up a pencil in order to write a grocery list or it can be an examination of a much deeper question as to the meaning of life.

Unless you are willing to examine the ***WHY*** behind your seemingly monotonous activities, both at work and outside of work, you will find yourself years from now in the same place, longing for change but not knowing what to do.

WHY has various tones that produce various outcomes. Your clear vision is your driving force, it's the purpose behind the moves you make. There is the inquisitive ***WHY*** from a 3-year-old that opens up worlds and understandings for the first time. While irritating, when you stop and really look at the question from a 3-year-old viewpoint, you can understand the curiosity behind the question.

I have had the great fortune to work as a leadership consultant for many manufacturing companies over the course of my career, and several of the processes I've learned and used in that industry are extremely helpful in many other areas, both professionally and personally.

The curious ***WHY*** shows up in those business processes with names like The Five Whys of Problem Solving or The Five Whys of Sales. Both of those can be traced to Total Quality Management (TQM) and Training Within Industry (TWI), and also problem-solving processes like Root Cause Analysis, all of which were developed to keep organizations productive and profitable.

As a Life Purpose and Career Coach, I have found the Five Why process to be extremely helpful in many circumstances. Here is an example of a Five Whys of Problem-Solving process, to help a coaching client with a career challenge.

(NOTE: although the root of every question is a "why," the process for getting there is less prescription and more conversation. Many times, in order to avoid the feeling of confrontation, I will word the question more as a request. Utilize the format and create your own specifics. Remember your desired outcome for each situation to which you apply the tool.)

Identify the problem or goal. I want to start my own business.

> *Why?* – I hate my job. (First why)
>
> *Why do you hate your job?* – I feel like my boss doesn't appreciate the work I do. (Second why)
>
> *Why does that upset you?* – Because it makes me want to prove to him that even if he doesn't see it, I am a valuable employee. (Third why)
>
> *Why is it important for you to care about the work you do?* – Because I when I lose interest at work, I take those feelings home with me. (Fourth why)
>
> *So why does the impact your work has on you at work and at home matter so much?* – Because there are probably lots of people who feel just like I do. I need to start my own business to help them find their own joy at work, so they can take that joy home instead of the frustration. (Fifth why, a root cause)

It's probably no surprise that that scenario was taken from my own experience at a former job. The frustration I felt at work was exactly what I needed in order to have the big why for starting my own business.

So, Root Cause is a very helpful way to get to the real problem and, consequently, a solution.

There is also a whining ***WHY*** that 3-year-olds can display when protesting bedtime or, really, proclaiming disgust over any directive. Adults can revert to this 3-year-old behavior themselves when they feel coerced against their own will. An associate of mine calls that "Sport Bitching," bitching for the sport of it. The tone

of voice that comes out in that version of the question proclaims very loudly where that person is on his evolutionary journey.

When the purpose behind the procedures or strategies is explained, it is often the clarity the question brings that is enough to shift out of a negative viewpoint. It's difficult to argue with your own idea, so when people are part of the solution, they generally give up being part of the problem .

Don't be afraid to question the seemingly rote way of doing a process. But be aware of the tone of voice you use when asking. Is it the whining ***WHY***? Or is it the sincerely curious ***WHY***?

Having the curiosity to question a long-standing process is one thing. Having the courage to ask the question of a person to whom it can have an impact may be another thing entirely.

When you have what you consider to be a good question and aren't sure how to ask it at work, be sure you've considered your intention for asking. Once you know what you stand for and are clear on your own WHY, the rest gets a lot easier.

Your Life Purpose

The question of life purpose is at the core of every human's experience in the world, whether they acknowledge it or not. For millennia, humans have asked the deep questions in pursuit of a broader experience of life.

Your gifts don't belong to you. They are entrusted to you for the benefit of the world.

When you listen to the yearnings of your heart and soul and really get in touch with SELF, not always listening to the louder voices that would try to talk you out of being still, you realize that you are a human being craving truth. When you are truthful with your own self, you realize that your deepest calling is to grow into your authentic selfhood.

Can you get to the light without having to go through the darkness? Maybe. Will you? Maybe not.

Each of us is led to our own truth and purpose by discovering and reconciling our weaknesses as much and as well as our strengths.

This is where the concept of gifts comes into play. All of us are gifted in our own specific ways. And those gifts are entrusted to us from our Creator. Unless we realize that they do not belong to us, we may be tempted to keep them to ourselves. Or to downplay them because they come easily to us.

I had the opportunity to coach a women's barbershop quartet as they were preparing for international competition. My area of expertise is not with the actual music, but with confidence and energetic projection.

One of the members of the quartet had won the international competition as a member of a previous quartet a few years before. She obviously knew what to do to win. As we began exploring each of the members' unique reasons for wanting to do the work needed to perform well at the competition, we dug a bit deeper into the concept of gifts and talents.

I remember saying to this international champion singer, "Remember, your gifts don't belong to you. They are entrusted to you for the benefit of the world. If you choose not to use them – in this case, it's your beautiful voice – you really are depriving the world of the opportunity to enjoy that gift."

I thought it was obvious. But apparently that touched a nerve for her. Tears sprang to her eyes, and it was as if she hadn't even thought about that before. Even someone as gifted as she had a blind spot in owning that gift.

It is important that we understand that with the light of our gifts comes the darkness of the shadow. For many people the shadow is the part of us we don't want to admit exists. It might be those traits and emotions we fear most in ourselves. Our gifts are easy to own. Our weaknesses and shadows, not so much. This does not mean we need to focus on our weaknesses and get better at them. On the contrary. As we recognize our own gifts, we also allow others to share their gifts. And then our weaknesses begin to fade. Our shadow, once acknowledged, gives way to the light of our true calling.

This is strikingly contrary to the way most of us were raised, and the way most of us learned within traditional settings. I'm certain our teachers and parents thought they were doing the right thing by blowing past the A's and concentrating more on how to bring the D's up. But since what you focus on expands, when

you take your eyes off the A's to struggle through the subjects you didn't like, you won't have much to report in the way of improvement.

Why should we be surprised that now, as adults in workplaces, we may be experiencing similar results when we focus on what's not working instead of celebrating strengths? The focus on competition that helped us win in high school sports has caused us now to lose out on other perspectives. Where business mentors and coaches talk about connecting and collaborating, we have no context because it goes against our conditioning.

Without realizing it, as we concentrated on what we needed to do to win over our competition, whether in sports or at work, we were experiencing the effects of fear to prevent, drive away, justify, push, manipulate, and get results at all costs. We didn't know there was another way.

To be sure, you may need fear to motivate you until love and faith inspire you.

But what if, instead of comparing and coming up short time and time again, you could go through the discernment process - discovering your gifts and your purpose - so that you could realize what you truly ***DESIRE***?

PURPOSE is really awareness. It's intent. It's knowing the end result, even if you don't know how you're going to get there. It's an experiment. It's being willing to take the risk to get the reward.

It's stepping into the specific external expression of the part of you that is unique.

I find myself doing most of the examining of my life while driving, and one morning I found myself pondering the subject of external validation.

On this particular Saturday morning on my way to my MasterMind group, I wondered why even as a supposedly responsible "adult," I still sometimes found myself seeking outside myself for approval or acceptance. I knew better, but that day I was noticing how often I'd made that mean more than it should.

For me the challenge was then, and probably still is at times, feeling what I feel without judgment. I remember as a kid and later as a young adult learning to stuff my feelings and think my way through every challenge. Consequently, I became a great thinker – but I lost some of my empathy regarding others and myself during those years.

It's interesting how selective my memory is when reflecting on that time in my life. I'm sure there were many and varied messages coming my way, but I seem to fixate on the memories of those comments that somehow implied I was wrong, or I shouldn't do or think or say or feel something I obviously felt compelled to do or think or say or feel. Why I gave up my own opinions to others during those years is beyond me now, but I did.

Now, with heightened awareness, I definitely KNOW better but don't always DO better. Thus, the dilemma.

Why do I still find myself at times looking for validation or appreciation or approval from people who can't - or don't know how - to give it? And why do I discount the many, many places I DO receive that appreciation and validation? And, the biggest question of all: why the need for external validation in the first place?

I'm a verbal processor, so I am a huge fan of MasterMinding: getting together on a regular basis with like-minded and like-hearted folks who I trust to listen objectively when I need to verbally process and give me honest feedback – and feedforward – when I request it (and even when I don't, but need it anyway!). It's not always easy for a recovering perfectionist to hear that I may not have it all figured out all the time, but that's what growth is all about.

Of course, the goal is to get to the point where questioning and processing is no longer necessary - to the point where knowing what I know is enough. But until that time, I'll trust that my own personal growth plan will give me more wisdom so that I can be the best coach and facilitator I can be. I understand that that is one of my gifts, and I just want to be able to provide that for more individuals and organizations - and be well compensated for it - so together we really can change the world.

As we improve our communication skills at work and at home, increasing numbers of us will get to that place of just knowing - where we don't have to work

Your purpose is not invented, it's discovered.

so hard to convince people of our point of view, but are open to learning from each other.

Often it's our shadow or our vulnerability that leads us most deeply into the discovery of our purpose. Looking outside for someone else to show the way to that inside treasure is like asking someone else for directions to a place they've never visited.

Instead of looking to others for answers, look to those likeminded others as companions on a similar journey to their own purpose. The MasterMind principle, as originally coined by Napoleon Hill, is what happens or emerges when people come together in a spirit of harmony for a definite purpose. The purpose of a MasterMind gathering, then, could be around a specific project or process, or the project could be discovering Life Purpose. In either case, it's a opportunity to live a more awakened and conscious life.

The process of waking up can be a slow one, but gratefully it's also a continuous one!

On Purpose and With Purpose

ON PURPOSE means not by accident. It's doing while being aware of the doing.

WITH PURPOSE means that meaning is applied intentionally.

Your purpose is not invented, it's discovered. It's your internal monitor. Your sixth sense. Your conscience. It's being a keen observer of the life you are

Without an **objective,** there is no **reason to start** any endeavor.

living, and recognizing that maybe your life is trying to live you instead. What is that gap?

Knowledge can lead to knowing, but you don't need knowledge to get to KNOWINGNESS.

In his classic book *Good to Great*, Jim Collins created a concept called the Hedgehog Concept, where a company was able to find the intersection of the three circles:

1. Understanding what your people are truly passionate about.
2. Identifying what the organization does better than anyone else.
3. Determining where it's good at generating revenue. (Collins calls this "understanding your economic engine.")

Before *Good to Great* was released, Collins did an interview with the founding editor of *Fast Company Magazine*, Alan Webber, where they talked about the findings of the research and applied it to individuals, not only corporations. The interview was gifted (on VHS tapes!) to readers of the magazine like I, who were part of their Company of Friends readers group.

In that interview, the three circles were altered a bit to be:

1. What you are passionate about and love to do;
2. What you were born to do;
3. What you can get paid to do.

I was very fortunate to discover my personal Hedgehog Concept as I used that tape with my career coaching clients, watching it over and over with them as they examined their own career paths, which allowed me to solidify my own at the same time.

Everything is an experiment, and it's much easier to duplicate results if you document. This is why journaling or MasterMinding is so crucial to lasting results.

As I suggested those activities for my clients, I did them myself. As a career coach, I learned that – no big surprise – there are lots of people who really have no idea exactly what they want for themselves and their lives. I could relate, so I'm more relatable.

Another tool I use in my coaching is *Think and Grow Rich* by Napoleon Hill. I have gotten to know that book very well over the years, and still study it several times a year as I continue to facilitate MasterMind study groups. (You will hear several references to *Think and Grow Rich* throughout this book because it has been a very significant inspiration for my work since I started studying it in 2007.)

Hill discovered that Desire, perhaps another way to identify Purpose, was one of the 13 principles of success he included in *Think and Grow Rich.*

In fact, Hill wrote that Desire is actually the starting point of all achievement. Without an objective, there is no reason to start any endeavor. You will only waste time and energy wandering aimlessly until you know your desired destination.

Unless you know better, you're probably going to find yourself living the life you chose years ago thanks to the conditioning you received from your earliest influences

like your parents and your teachers. After all, you were an impressionable little dude or dudette way back when.

But now, as a responsible adult, unless you change direction, don't be surprised when you end up exactly where you are headed.

That's probability.

But for the purposes of our conversation here, we're going to ask you to veer from probability and venture into the realm of possibility. That's another concept altogether.

Possibility implies opportunity; probability is stuck energy.

Even if it's tiny, when the possibility exists for something hoped for, the outcome you truly desire has a way of presenting itself.

To review, purpose is the answer to the question why. Take a look at some of the sacred cows in your organization and in your life and put them to the WHY test. If you're only doing something because it's the way you've always done it, or if you're not doing something either because you tried it before and it didn't work or you've never done it that way before, now might be the time to revisit it.

When individuals inside organizations don't feel safe questioning a procedure or a strategy, there's more going on behind the question.

Why don't people feel safe? What keeps them from being honest? What is the reason we never __________ or we always ______________?

When people are part of the solution, they won't feel the need to keep the problem going. And sometimes it's as simple as knowing the why.

TOOLS for DISCOVERING PURPOSE

Conversational Tools:

In response to a statement like: "I don't know what to do."
I know you don't know, but if you did, what would it be?

In response to a complaint:
OK. I get that you don't like that /want that /accept that. What do you want instead?

In response to a suggestion:
That's a great idea. Would you be interested in helping me flesh it out?

In response to a compliment:
Thank you! I really appreciate you noticing/recognizing/saying that. That means a lot to me.

In response to a whining WHY question:
Is this a question to which you are seeking a solution, or do you just need to vent? Is this a 5-Why WHY or a Sport-bitching WHY?

Experiential Tools:

The results these tools produce will be best measured by recording observations in a small notebook or journal. Choose one of the following "assignments" each week and share observations in weekly team meetings or with a MasterMind group.

Notice What You Notice. Set the intention at the beginning of the week, and record observations. What grabs your attention enough so that you feel called to record that? Scan your environment without judging, and just notice.

Make a "Don't Want" List. As humans we have been conditioned from an early age to be very clear about what we don't want in our lives. Babies are told "NO" many, many times more than they are told "YES" during their formative years. So, get serious about creating your list. Draw a vertical line the down middle of the pages of your notebook where you will record this list. Write on the left side of the middle line.

Change Your "Don't Want" List to the Exact Opposite. Now that you've determined with some clarity and certainty what you don't want to have, become, or experience, for each "don't" statement, write the exact opposite on the right side of the page. Share with your team which list was easier to make, and which one was the most fun. What do you notice about your language from this exercise?

Values Vote. Do you know your core values? If you're like most people you might have an idea, but you haven't really solidified them. Here's your chance. This will take some time and focus, but what you will find when you take that time and focus is that you either are or are not living your life on purpose by your values. This exercise is valuable for your whole life, and also for your career. For more information and a list of possible values, visit our website: www.powertoolsatwork.com/tools

What's On Your Plate? Hand out round paper plates to everyone and have them write/draw what's currently "on their plate." How do they see their lives and activities? This is a great way to discover why some of us feel overwhelmed and stressed. There's a lot on our plates. It's also interesting to see how others arrange their plates when drawing or writing, and how they present this information to others. You may discover that there are some things on your plate that really need to be taken off: either stop doing them or delegate them.

Create Team Memes. Memes are all the rage right now and it's fun to discover what we find interesting, inspiring, funny, and even a little edgy. Use a software like www.canva.com to help you with your creation and use the memes on your teams to lighten the mood or to remind each other of specific ideas, unique culture pieces or even inside jokes.

Distribute liberally; make sure to include everyone. Never make a meme about someone else without their permission and knowledge. Remember: the definition of gossip is speaking negatively about someone who is not present.

Celebrate Gifts. Back in ancient history, Aristotle discovered that what men and women most want in their experience of life is to be happy. That's not such a startling fact to most of us. But when do you feel the most happy? True happiness never depends on outside events or conditions, it depends on how we interpret those conditions. It's not what happens to us, it's who we become. In his book *Flow: The Psychology of Optimal Experience,* Mihaly Csikszentmihalyi tells us that "the best moments in our lives usually occur when our bodies or minds are stretched to the limits in a voluntary effort to accomplish something difficult and worthwhile."[1]

What are you doing when you are in the flow state? When the experience you're in as a result of your hard work and dedication just seems easy? Ask a close friend, colleague or family member what they see as your gifts. Consider these questions from *Is Your Genius At Work,* by Dick Richards for yourself (or use them in dialogue to help each other discover your gifts):

- What do you consistently attempt to give to others?
- What are others seeking when they come to you?

- What activities do you enjoy solely for their own sake?
- Describe a time when you were successful.
- Describe a time when you felt good about yourself.
- Describe a time when things just seemed to flow naturally.[2]

When you uncover and claim your gifts, you may believe that everyone can do what comes naturally and easily to you. You may even discount them as unimportant. But allowing someone else to notice what s/he notices about you will help you see that perhaps it's easy for you because it's a gift. Develop an attitude of gratitude for those characteristics and talents that seem easy to you, yet which others see as valuable to them and the world.

Write Your Manifesto. A manifesto is a public declaration of principles and intentions. It may be life-stance related. A person's life stance is his or her relation with what he or she accepts as of ultimate importance, and includes the commitment and practice of working it out in living. This is not a mission statement for a wall or a T-shirt, but a way of being.

What principles guide the living of your life?

As an example only, here are a couple of bullet points from my manifesto:

- Every single person, no matter what title or position, has the capacity to turn any organization into a more positive, productive community.
- Until we know something, we cannot take a new action.
- There is a point at which people at any level of an organization must choose new approaches to create new results.
- Our value as leaders does not exist in what we have done or even in what we may do; it exists in who we are being now.
- No behavior or technique "out there" will produce new results until we become clear what's going on "in here."

Write Your Six-Word Memoir. Less is more, as they say (whoever *they* are!). So if you were to break down your essence into only six words, what story would that tell about you and your life?

This idea was inspired by a legend that writer Ernest Hemingway was challenged to write a novel in six words. His novel: "For Sale: Baby Shoes. Never Worn."

According to an online NPR article[3], Smith Magazine invited writers "famous and obscure" to

distill their own life stories into exactly six words. *It All Changed in an Instant* is the fourth collection of very, very brief life stories from *Smith*.

Here are a few examples:

Alzheimer's: meeting new people every day.
Phil Skversky

Met wife at her bachelorette party.
Eddie Matz

Family portrait: everyone smiles but me.
Ian Baaske

Full circle: morgue tech becomes obstetrician.
Andrea Skorenki

So would you believe me anyway?
James Frey

Go ahead. Try it for yourself, and then share with those in your life.

Determine Your Flag on the Mountain. If you consider your work life as a trek up a mountain, what would be the flag you would want to plant at the top? What is the biggest reason you are working at all? Paying the bills is not it. There must a bigger reason for your flag. Is it a trip to Guadalajara? Is it braces for your son? Is it a private school? Have everyone on your team create a paper pennant with their destination written on it. Then pin it on a paper mountain in the break room

or somewhere everyone can see it. Then ask each other "How are we doing getting you to Guadalajara?" When you have a destination in mind, it's easier to remember why you are doing what you are doing to get there.

What Do You Want Instead? Notice which situations in your home, your work, or the world get you agitated. Where do you feel that agitation? In your shoulders? Your jaw? Your stomach? Instead of allowing this physical information to get the best of you, regain the best of you by asking yourself, "OK, Self, what do I want instead?"

When you get clear about what your desired outcome would be, you can then decide whether you're committed to doing what it would take to create that outcome or just interested. Usually just that distinction will allow you to let go of the angst.

Like a Snapchat filter, try this one with someone to get even greater impact and insight.

Celebrate Something Unexpected. Look around your home, work, community, world. What is something you see there that you never noticed before? Is it a physical landmark you've driven by hundreds of times but just never paid attention? Is it a brightly colored garden flag you noticed in someone's yard while on your walk? Is it a photo on someone's desk? Find a reason to point it out and then, with the help of the person you mentioned it to, plan a random celebration.

Marlo Anderson is a native North Dakotan who just decided to create the National Day Calendar back in 2013. Here are some really cool facts from his Wikipedia site:

On January 19, 2013, Anderson founded the *National Day Calendar*. The site quickly became a popular destination for media wanting to know more about how the National Days came to be. Anderson's team has also been responsible for creating close to 200 new National Days including *National Astronaut Day* and *National Bobblehead Day*. Over 20,000 media outlets and personalities follow Anderson's daily post and use his content as prep for their daily shows. *National Day Calendar* has turned unknown holidays such as *National Pizza Day* and *National Coffee Day* into the top trending topics of all time on Social Media. Anderson has also been featured in articles that discuss the effect his trend has on the national economy. Even the Chinese retailer Alibaba has capitalized on Singles' Day by promoting it in their marketing as a day to buy something for themselves. By leveraging this trending topic on its own site, Alibaba boasted sales of $17.8 billion in 2016.[4]

All of that to tell you that if Anderson can make this big an impact, so can you. Live by his motto: "Celebrate Every Day."

Questioning Up. First ask yourself the same questions you'd like to ask of your manager or supervisor - and do your best to think about the question from his/her perspective.

Try these (or similar questions):

"Why are certain procedures and practices in place? Why is that old equipment still in use? What might be the benefits and costs of making a change (to policies or equipment)—and how difficult would it be to do that?"

Having thought about these issues, and gathered some relevant facts, you can then ask questions that are more informed, empathetic, and practical. The question you ask should be framed less as a gripe and more as a possibility you've thought about and would like to explore further.

Try this: **"I've noticed that our competitors are using new software that allows them to move more quickly. I understand the software may be really expensive, but I'm wondering about some of the other ways we could respond—and whether there's anything specific that I can do differently in my role?"**

When "questioning up," one of the best ways to show respect—and to learn important information from managers—is to ask for advice. Most people are honored when you ask them for advice, and managers

are no exception. When you ask a manager for advice, you're often making her job a little easier—because you're providing a welcome opening for that manager to give you constructive criticism.[5]

Make Team Agreements. Be committed to finding the WHY behind the policies and standards you establish for team harmony. Ray Dalio, in his book *Principles,* describes the standards he has established for his organization. He calls the principles which guide his team "agreements" for how to be and how to handle specific situations.

These are three of the agreements for his organization:

1) Be radically honest with each other.

2) Be willing to have thoughtful disagreements, or what I would call dialogues, where everyone can learn from each other.

3) Establish agreed-upon standards for any lingering disagreements so they don't turn into resentments.[6]

In order to provide the most positive outcome for those agreements, be sure your team has established its desired shared outcomes. Know your team commitments, which are situations where you are willing to do whatever it takes, even when the emotion you were in when you created them wears off, and may be overtaken by emotion in the moment when you most need to lean on those commitments.

1 Mihaly Csikszentmihalyi, *Flow: The Psychology of Optimal Experience,* (New York: Harper Perennial, 1990), p.3.
2 Dick Richards, *Is Your Genius At Work? 4 Key Questions to Ask Before Your Next Career Move,* (Mountain View, California: Davies-Black Publishing, 2005), pp. 128-129.
3 https://www.npr.org/templates/story/story.php?storyId=123289019
4 https://en.wikipedia.org/wiki/Marlo_Anderson
5 http://amorebeautifulquestion.com/how-it-can-help-you-to-ask-questions-at-work/
6 Ray Dalio, *Principles,* (New York: Simon & Schuster Audio, 2017).

Part 2: OPEN MINDEDNESS

Your Invitation to Lifelong Learning

Have you ever seen those cash booths at trade shows or events? These money machines look like old-fashioned phone booths, but they are filled with cash that is being blown around inside.

It's hard to miss the excitement the cash booth creates as people step inside and do their best to snatch as much cash as they can in their allotted timeframe.

If you've ever witnessed this spectacle, you notice that the lucky participants don't just grab one handful of cash. They are frantically stuffing money into their pockets, shirts, pants - anywhere they can so they are free to grab more.

How much money would they gather if they were not willing to part with the cash in hand on the first grab? They have to be willing to open their hands in order to be able to grab more.

How much information or knowledge can you gather if you are not willing to

open your mind

to learn more than you already know ?

Think of your mind like the fist in this example. How much information or knowledge can you gather and accumulate if you are not willing to open your mind to learn more than you already know ?

Let's take that one step further. That open mind would need some sort of gatekeeper to sort through the positive and the negative: the experiences and opportunities you desire and those you don't. That gatekeeper would need to be directed so it would know which types of thoughts to allow and which to block. So it would operate as a thermostat does.

A thermostat sets the temperature of a room, and it kicks in when the temperature deviates from the set point. Your mindset does the same thing for your attitude. When you set your mind toward what you do want instead of away from what you don't, you have the ability to experience the effects your positive – or your negative – set point will produce.

Stanford University professor and author Dr. Carol Dweck is one of the world's foremost experts in the field of psychological mindset.

In her research, Dweck has discovered that everyone has one of two basic mindsets: fixed or growth.

If you have a fixed mindset, you believe that your talents and abilities are set in stone – either you have them or you don't. You must prove yourself over and over, trying to look smart and talented at all costs. This is the path of stagnation.

If you have a growth mindset, however, you know that talents can be developed and that great abilities are built over time. This is the path of opportunity – and success.

The implication in Dweck's work used to be that whether or not you had a tendency toward growth or fixed mindset, growth was the "right" choice and you could either rest on your growth-mindset laurels or force yourself to away from your fixed mindset into the land of growth.

Over time Dweck has begun to shift her outlook. In a 2015 commentary on Education Week's website, Dweck wrote:

> *"Let's legitimize the fixed mindset. Let's acknowledge that (1) we're all a mixture of fixed and growth mindsets, (2) we will probably always be, and (3) if we want to move closer to a growth mindset in our thoughts and practices, we need to stay in touch with our fixed-mindset thoughts and deeds.*
>
> *"If we 'ban' the fixed mindset, we will surely create false growth-mindsets. (By the way, I also fear that if we use mindset measures for accountability, we will create false growth mindsets on an unprecedented scale.) But if we watch carefully for our fixed-mindset triggers, we can begin the true journey to a growth mindset."*[1]

Being open-minded does not mean being empty-headed. It means being coachable. There is an inherent danger of the success that can be experienced through extreme coachability, however. Take a sport like basketball.

On the court, a player has a definite outcome in mind. That outcome is to score more points than the other team does.

The problem with success in an area like athletics is that the more successful competitive athletes get over time, the more likely they become less open and less coachable. They tend to believe that their current status is all that matters, and they may very well hold tightly to that one and only winning formula.

This is not only relevant in basketball, but in life. Leadership coach and author Marshall Goldsmith even wrote a book he titled *What Got You Here Won't Get You There*. Although he has written 35 books, this one is a Wall Street Journal #1 business book and winner of the Harold Longman Award for Business Book of the Year. CEOs who hire Goldsmith for one-on-one coaching pay him $250,000 for that privilege. He must be on to something.

There is danger in holding onto a winning formula because it is a sure sign of a fixed mindset. Once you think you know it all, you're doomed to be as smart as you're ever going to be. If you are the smartest person in the room, you're in the wrong room .

A truly open-minded person forwards the action – moves the ball down the field or court, knowing that if he/she needs to go back, it's ultimately to move forward.

When you are open-minded, you are willing to learn and to share your learning. You are also willing to admit what you don't know.

Being open allows questions even if there are no answers. It's more about the space to question, not about being right about the answers.

Unless you are open to new possibilities, you will always get what you've always gotten Don't be surprised when nothing changes.

The opposite, then, of open and coachable might be cynical and resigned. The gatekeeper keeping watch over that fixed mindset is programmed to keep out new ideas. If the only experiences you are presented, then, are those you already understand and judge as the "right" options, it's no wonder that being right about everything being wrong is an understandable pathway to upset and resignation.

You can't distinguish your filters unless you are aware of them. You will end up swimming in the water of your own opinions. The danger comes when you believe your opinions are THE truth.

Openness allows for thoughts you've never had before to become reality. What is your truth? What are you willing to stand for? Could there be other perspectives? Might there be other ways to see the world than through the narrow focus you've seen it?

This realization might be painful at first. It will take courage not to be discouraged.

Once you open your mind to seeing situations and people differently, you will begin to realize that most people don't know what they don't know. That boss with whom you can't seem to get along – the one who thinks his is the only right answer? Maybe he's speaking and lashing out from his own brokenness. Maybe he's not avoiding you because he thinks you have nothing important to add, but because he realizes deep down that you do ... and if he really listens to your logic, he may be forced to change his opinion. He may only have a need to be right about everything so he doesn't have to admit to having been wrong.

You won't know whether that perspective is a story you've made up in your head or if it's true unless you are willing to have that conversation with people like your boss. Whether you choose to check your hunch or not, just considering it will open your mind – and your heart – to a possibility that didn't exist when you were trying to convince him to be more open.

The questions that occur to you are the most important ones. If you're only listening to people who think like you to prove that what you already know is justified, you will never be open to learning. You will never create space for others to share and be vulnerable and learn to trust. Your past experience will keep you from expanding.

It is when you
don't know
the how
of something
that your
willingness
or your
WON'Tingness
will kick in.

It will be up to you to bring your own questions to the light or you will remain in the dark.

This whole concept of open-mindedness, then, might be thought of as a gradual dawning; the light eventually shining away the darkness a fixed mindset perpetuates. And it's not enough to only believe in the possibility of stepping out of the dark. You don't learn by only observing, you truly learn by participating.

To have a breakthrough, identify the barriers. Shine the light. Be open to the possibility that there is always more to know.

Once you notice the opportunity that shifting to a more open mindset can make available, be willing to do whatever it takes to experience that openness. Your willingness is the key. No one else's how-to guide will ever help you succeed if you are not open to taking the risk of getting uncomfortable. In fact, it is exactly when you ***don't*** know the how of something that your willingness (or your WON'Tingness) will kick in.

The really counterintuitive part about being **OPEN** and **WILLING** is that there is no actual **DOING** required. It's not the **DOING** that counts, it's the **OPENNESS** and **WILLINGNESS** that does.

Many people are so addicted to doing that they beat themselves up when they're not doing enough. That's what is working against us in the modern western world. We are busy and not productive. We keep our minds occupied so we won't have to dig in

Once you identify your longing **to be** at a different level of **connectedness** and **possibility**, you won't be content staying on the surface.

and discover what's truly important and crucial to our individual success (however we define it).

In fact, you are probably ***doing*** against your inner ***being*** because you haven't stopped long enough to discover what you truly desire. Your calling is waiting for you to be quiet enough to hear it and you spend most of your life drowning it out and then being right about how your life is unfulfilling.

It's there, right below the surface, just waiting for you to discover it.

As you dive in, you will see that following the depth is more valuable than staying on the surface.

Once you identify your longing to ***be*** at a different level of connectedness and possibility, you won't be content staying on the surface.

In the 2018 remake of ***A Star is Born***, Lady Gaga showed amazing depth as she took on the lead role of Ally, and also showed her own vulnerability as an artist with her original song from the movie. If you haven't listened and processed the lyrics, take a look here and then go find the song. It will take you to a new place and you will feel the impact of being open in a new way.

SHALLOW

Performed by Lady Gaga, Bradley Cooper

Tell me somethin', girl
Are you happy in this modern world?
Or do you need more?
Is there somethin' else you're searchin' for?
I'm falling
In all the good times I find myself
Longin' for change
And in the bad times I fear myself
Tell me something, boy
Aren't you tired tryin' to fill that void?
Or do you need more?
Ain't it hard keeping it so hardcore?
I'm falling
In all the good times I find myself
Longing for change
And in the bad times I fear myself
I'm off the deep end, watch as I dive in
I'll never meet the ground
Crash through the surface, where they can't hurt us
We're far from the shallow now
In the shallow, shallow
In the shallow, shallow
In the shallow, shallow

Songwriters: Andrew Wyatt / Anthony Rossomando / Mark Ronson / Stefani Germanotta

When you really understand the concept of OPEN-MINDEDNESS, you realize that the most important part of your ***doing*** is actually in your ***being***. If you decided what you really want to ***be*** (like your parents asked you when you were little: What do you want to ***be*** when you grow up?) you didn't think about what a fireman would ***do***, you only thought about ***being*** that. It never occurred to you to think about what a racecar driver or a pro football player or a ballerina would need to ***do*** in order to ***be*** a football player or ballerina ... only the end result. Without realizing it, as kids we were only connected with the feeling associated with ***being*** the person who would have the title or position.

Then we grew up and realized that there's no such thing as something for nothing. We were taught and conditioned that you need to work hard to pay the price to become worthy of having the possibility of maybe someday being happy or successful or peaceful.

The reality, however, is quite different from your early conditioning. Instead of HAVE DO BE, it's actually completely reversed.

Decide first what you want to BE and then DO what you do from that space. When you do that, you will realize that you already HAVE everything you need.

1 https://www.edweek.org/ew/articles/2015/09/23/carol-dweck-revisits-the-growth-mindset.html

Decide first what you
want to BE
and then
DO what you do
from **that** space.

When you do that,
you will realize that
you already
HAVE
everything you need.

TOOLS for BECOMING OPEN-MINDED

Conversational Tools:

In response to a statement like: "I haven't done this before."
Neither have I. It can be scary. I've got your back. You're not alone.

In response to a complaint:
Have I not been clear in the vision? Please help me set the stage better. With more information, does that change your outlook?

In response to a suggestion:
Tell me more. Help me understand your desired outcome and what you envision.

In response to a compliment:
Thank you! I'm glad you are on board with this idea and recognize where we could go.

Experiential Tools:

The results these tools produce will be best measured by recording observations in a small notebook or journal. Choose one of the following "assignments" each week and share observations in weekly team meetings.

Give What You Most Want. For the next week, make it a point to give to someone else something you most want. If it's money you want, give some. If it's respect, give that. Whatever you most want, give it to someone else. Record what you notice and how you feel.

Invite to the White. This tool is inspired by Susan Scott in her book *Fierce Conversations*. Picture a big beach ball with different colored stripes. Now imagine the white circle on the end of the ball where you blow it up. Got that picture in your mind? Now imagine that your perspective is the blue stripe on the ball. It's where you live, where you've come from, what you do without even thinking. To you, the world is blue.

Remember, as you share your blueness with whoever will listen, that someone else in your life - whether at work or at home - also has his/her own perspective. That someone else might see the world on the yellow stripe. He is steeped in yellow all day long, and it's because he was born and raised in yellow.

The same is true for the red, the green, and every other color on the ball.

Because you are the one reading this book, it is now your responsibility to invite everyone to consider the white circle where all the colors come together. Invite to the White. On the white circle, no one's color is better than anyone else's. There is no position or title or tenure on the White.

On the White, we are engaged in dialogue – suspending previous assumptions in order to learn from each other.

How does that analogy shift your perception of the world?

Ask Instead of Tell. Tone of voice is a huge part of the delivery of any message. In fact, research shows that 38% of the effectiveness of any message comes from the rate, the speed, the pitch of your voice. And telling someone something generally brings with it a declarative tone that might suggest you're not open to dialogue.

Instead of giving a command or telling your own story or perspective, ask a question of the other person. If you're in sales, you've probably been told it's important to "close the sale." In "closing," whether it's a sale or a dialogue, that's the end of story. No more opportunity.

Instead of closing, consider opening the relationship. Asking opens, telling closes.

Remember, too, that you can't fake sincerity no matter how hard you try. People can sniff out a technique or a manipulation miles away. If you are clear about your desired outcome and it truly is to open a relationship, your questions will come naturally. Let your curiosity guide you.

Listen to a New Radio Station. This week, instead of your regular radio station, pick a new one. If you're a country fan, listen to jazz. If you're into talk radio, see if you can tune into a program with a different point of view. Even if you have the music or talk on in the background, it is still making its way into your subconscious. It's no shock that upbeat music keeps you motivated. Try soft and mellow sounds to help you focus on your work. Ambient music, like background soundtracks or elevator music will help when you're stressed. If you're feeling tired and uninspired at work, try epic music - adventure movie soundtracks, for example.

Nature sounds like waterfalls or rainfall can help enhance concentration. Just beware of chirping birds or other noises you're not expecting. They can be a bit jarring. Baroque music has been found to increase mood and concentration for doctors on the job.

Experiment and see what works. Soft and mellow may help you to focus on your work, while a high energy piece can keep you motivated. Don't be afraid, too, to allow the silence to make the moment golden.

Horriblizing. You already do this without realizing it when you find yourself in fear of making a decision, so let's go there. Really dig in. What's the worst thing that could happen? What's the worst thing someone would ever say about you? Do to you? What's the absolute worst thing? Now that you've gone there in your mind, it will never seem that scary in real life. Use this process with a team and watch the conversation go from fearful to funny in just a few minutes.

Person or Object. One of the most dangerous points of view that can take hold of people is self-deception. As soon as you make a decision that goes against what you know to be the right thing, you will find yourself justifying your decision. Train yourself to notice when you start treating people as objects that either get in your way, or that you can use for your own gain. If you remember that any person in your life, no matter who he is or how much she upsets you, is a PERSON, not an OBJECT, you have the ability to shift your thinking and take different action.

I Wonder If. Unless you are willing and able to check a hunch you have about someone else's behavior or language, you will be making up a story in your own head. Any time you find yourself thinking or saying "I bet he ..." or "I wonder if she ..." or "he probably ..." it's a pretty good bet that you are making up a story. Unless you catch yourself at the beginning of this discovery phase, you might find yourself actually believing the story you've made up, and will do everything you can to find evidence to prove you are right. Instead, stop and question your own outlook. Never jump to conclusions. Dig deep to find the facts and check your hunches.

Write With Your Opposite Hand. When I played basketball, I understood the benefit of developing my non-dominant hand. But that was years and years ago. Looking back now I see how concentrating on building that skill still impacts me today. Using your opposite hand will strengthen neural connections in your brain, and even grow new ones. It's similar to how physical exercise improves your body's functioning and grows muscles.

Try using your non-dominant hand to write. Use it to control the computer mouse or television remote. Brush your teeth with your other hand. You'll probably notice it's much harder to be precise with your movements at first, but if you stick with it, you will see improvements.

This process builds your creativity and will also give you a new perspective about other processes people need to learn or relearn as the result of injury, or even what your toddler may go through as she develops fine motor skills.

I'm naturally right-handed, but I realize now that perhaps the reason I deal cards with my left hand and steer my car more naturally with my left hand might have to do with that opportunity I opened up during my basketball days.

Wedge Exercise. You will need a large open space and some masking tape. Section the floor of an open space into 8 wedges or slices of pie by putting down masking tape. Make sure the wedges are large enough for a couple of people to stand inside of. Print these labels on letter-sized paper, big enough to fill the page. The labels are: BIG CHICKEN. I AM A STAR. ALWAYS LATE. OUT ON A LIMB. TEDIOUS AND ROUTINE. PASSIONATE AND ADVENTUROUS. DEEP DARK HOLE. Ask participants to space themselves evenly inside the wedges so they are physically standing in the space. Now place one of the labels on the floor in each of the wedges. Allow the participants to really feel the feeling of standing in that space. Randomly call out one of the labels and ask the participants in that wedge how it feels to be what that labels calls them.

You can modify this exercise if people are seated at round tables by placing the labels in the center of the tables. Be sure to have enough labels for the number of tables. Instead of having the participants move, just switch out the labels to give them different experiences.

The dialogue created by this exercise often helps participants see that the process of stepping into the space, even figuratively, can help get a different perspective about the way others think and act.

No Naming. Spend some time in the presence of something you consider beautiful – a flower, a gem, a piece of artwork. As you look at the object, try to see it without naming it mentally. When we appreciate beauty this way, a window opens into the formless and into a state of gratitude. See if you can experience that. Note your observations in your journal (From Oprah's online study guide for Eckhart Tolle's *A New Earth*).

Play the "What If" game. Come up with a list of "what-if" questions and then finish the questions with some contrary-to-fact condition, idea or situation. The what-if question can be whatever you wish, just as long as it is not a currently existing situation. The nice thing about "what-iffing" is that it allows you to suspend a few rules and assumptions, and get into a germinal frame of mind. Examples:

- What if animals become more intelligent than people?
- What if human life-expectancy were 200 years?
- What if everything you touched turned to chocolate?
- What if everybody in your company played a musical instrument, and you had a concert every Friday afternoon at 3:00?
- What if there were no clocks? How would you know how long to stay at work?
- What if we had seven fingers on each hand?

Now answer the question.

You can find a large bank of what-if questions on our website: http://www.powertoolsatwork.com/tools

Ask yourself,

What keeps happening

FOR

me?

Part Three: WISDOM

Looking Back to Go Forward

Words create worlds.

What have you learned throughout the history (or herstory) of you?

The stories you're telling yourself about people, situations, and even yourself are from the past. Until you know that, you are lost in the story and you start to see the future from that story.

"What keeps happening ***TO*** me" is a story. And the best (and worst) thing about that story is that you always get to be right.

Wisdom is tapping into the flipped script of that story and asking "What keeps happening ***FOR*** me?"

The truth is that the universe/God/infinite intelligence is sending signals every day. Every minute, really. Those signals occur as messages. That message might be like a breeze blowing by your cheek. Or all

Wisdom comes from hindsight and it's always 20/20.

the traffic signals turning green (or red!). Or seeing a hummingbird. Or a feather. It might be so subtle you don't even notice it. But it's still there.

If you don't get the message, you'll be presented with a lesson. You'll have an opportunity to learn and redirect. It will be more like a tap on the shoulder. Maybe someone literally bumps into you when you are walking and texting. Or you experience a near-miss at your workplace (side note: why is it called a near miss? Wouldn't that imply that it hit? Shouldn't it be a near-hit instead? But we digress ...)

If you miss the lesson and just go back to doing your life without acknowledging it, you'll be presented with a problem. This will be like a shove against the wall. Maybe you have a fender bender while you're driving (notice if you get hit from the back or from the front. Both have lessons to deliver). Or you lose or break something of value to you. All of these are stronger signals working to wake you up and redirect your activities toward what you do want instead of away from what you don't.

If the problem doesn't wake you up, you'll be presented with a crisis. This is like getting run over by a steamroller. You have a heart attack. Your house is broken into. You are forced to file bankruptcy.

Of course, you can only connect the dots looking backward. Wisdom comes from hindsight and it's always 20/20. But you can never retract a word once it's spoken and you can never regain a lost opportunity.

Unless you change direction, you will end up where you are headed.

You can, however, use your new wisdom to alter who you decide to be right now, in the moment.

The future is really created for you in the moment you decide on your burning desire and put a pin in the proverbial map of your life looking forward from today. Unless you change direction, you will end up where you are headed. And unless that's exactly what's on your life plan, now would be a good time to alter your probable future.

Wisdom is the ability to understand and utilize the laws of nature, so that instead of being at their mercy, you can have them work for you. It is knowing what you know as well as what you don't know. It's a result of experience, not theory.

You want your kids to learn from your mistakes so they don't have to live through them, but the best result they can expect is to grow in theory, not in practical application. Think of everything you ever got in trouble for doing as a kid. Now think about those things you did, but didn't get caught. Would you trade the learning you got from those experiences? Your kids will learn, too. Everyone has his or her own journey. Ever wonder why your parents got wiser the older YOU got?

Think about wisdom like this. There's a map and there's the actual road. The map only tells you ABOUT the route, and even though a GPS can tell you a little more detail with a little less hassle, it's still only telling you ABOUT the current situation. You

still won't physically observe and experience the road construction or the traffic jam until you get into it - or until you recalculate and avoid it.

It's only theory until it's reality.

Thinking allows you to build knowledge, and knowledge is limited to rational thought. But when you tap into your experiential observation, you have access to wisdom, which is very individualized. You can certainly share your wisdom, and when you do that from an open-minded perspective, it becomes less about a ***SHOULD*** and more about a ***SHARE***.

Modeling that individual choice has a distinct effect from force which often produces resistance and collusion, even though it sometimes seems like a good choice to save others from the trouble of their own experience.

Navigating a subject - or a road - with only knowledge and no experience might give the person a slight advantage over someone who has no knowledge, but it will be more difficult to tap into the intuition that is developed as a result of experience.

On the other hand, the person with experience but no knowledge would intuitively manage the road and directions but wouldn't be able to tell someone else how to follow those directions.

Teaching or trying to tell someone else about wisdom in order to help them avoid their own experience is a very odd circumstance when you really break it down.

Knowledge vs. Wisdom

Knowledge and wisdom, then, are two distinct concepts. Knowledge can help with wisdom, but knowledge is not required for building experience.

As humans, we have the ability to learn - to accumulate knowledge, which is important, but insight without action builds no wisdom. That ability is built through interaction and adaptation to our ever-changing reality.

Prior experience, mistakes, and lessons continue to add to wisdom, and allow you to just KNOW what to do without having to ask permission or check with the rules of knowledge. Thus, KNOWING and KNOWLEDGE are also separate entities. No one can possibly accumulate another's wisdom. Nothing external can save a person the trouble or give the knowing unless he/she has actually driven the route.

Studying geology, civil engineering, theory of urban planning, and the nature of traffic patterns will certainly help one grow in knowledge, but it's what one chooses to do with this knowledge that will have the greatest impact.

People who are book smart may appear to have an advantage, especially in our traditional hierarchical corporate structure of business and even education.

But if a person thinks he knows more than another, he will not be willing to hear someone else's wisdom and experience, and he will be destined to remain only as wise as he currently is.

Wisdom tends to broaden and deepen with time and with age. Sometimes language fails us when we attempt to share an experience, so impatience is a barrier to connection.

Whatever side you are on for any issue that has sides, you will generally take your position based on your own unique bias and perspective, usually because of your own experience.

Rationally, things make sense or they don't. But humans are not always rational, and wisdom doesn't work that way anyway. People are complex, and other peoples' experience and knowledge mess with our own and make it even more messy and complex. When we remember the purpose or objective or desired outcome for any action we take, and stay open-minded as we give and receive counsel and advice, we grow in wisdom and realize, over time, that being right may not be our only option.

While wisdom doesn't have to mean age, and getting older doesn't automatically mean getting wiser, you might miss out on opportunities if you're not at least curious about the wisdom of those with longevity inside the corporate structure.

In his book *Wisdom @ Work: The Making of a Modern Elder*, Chip Conley, Strategic Advisor for Hospitality and Strategy at Airbnb, has advice for any organization looking to have a significant impact.

"This is the perfect time for elders to make a comeback," he says, "thanks to their ability to

synthesize wise, empathetic solutions that no robot could ever imagine. In an era of machine intelligence, emotional intelligence and empathy—something older people have in spades—are more valuable than ever. The more high-tech we become, the more high touch we desire." [1]

Because you seem to lose some of your inhibitions and gain self-confidence as you get older, you tend to take more risks, especially in the area of interpersonal communication. It finally makes sense that what other people think of you is none of your business and you somehow feel freer to be authentic and vulnerable with those workplace relationships.

At this point it makes some sense to either offer your wisdom, or tap into the wisdom of those of your co-workers and mentors on a formal or an informal basis. MasterMind groups, book studies, think tanks, peer councils and mentorship opportunities are great ways to match newer and more experienced workers to share experiences and points of view.

What can each of us learn from our experiences? If all of life is a continual opportunity to get it better than the day before, what was the biggest lesson from yesterday?

What you choose to do with the experience and wisdom you have accumulated is entirely up to you. But if you will stop and think for a moment about all the experiences and opportunities you have been given throughout your entire life, wouldn't it be foolish to waste them making the same mistakes that got you here?

It's how you **connect** and **employ** **knowledge** that counts.

Wisdom makes knowledge effective.

It is only with the expanding perspective that maturity brings, that you can begin to develop wisdom. And opinion is not wisdom.

You do not gain wisdom from reading a book. On the other hand, you *can* begin to develop it from the knowledge gained from careful observation of the lives of others, from critical examination of your own life, and from purposeful meditation. It's how you connect and employ knowledge that counts. Wisdom makes knowledge effective. Without wisdom you cannot really benefit from what you know.

Often learning through your mistakes or your most painful experiences is worth the price you have to pay to go through them.

Over the course of my career, and only in hindsight, can I see that the common denominator in all my toughest situations was me. Not a huge surprise, but at the time, I just couldn't see it.

As I worked through some of my own growth opportunities (that sounds so much better than "weaknesses," doesn't it?), it seemed so unfortunate that I kept finding myself in work situations where my boss or immediate supervisor just didn't get me.

I offered what I thought were very good suggestions and, on more than one occasion and in more than one specific job, my suggestions were either ignored, discounted, or, in one case, passed off as the boss's (yes, it does happen in real life!).

I just couldn't understand why these people were not seeing the value I brought to the organization, so I continued to leave one job to go to another, only to find the same thing happening again.

Was I unlucky? Or was I consistent? Working through my own experiences, I realize that the consistency I thought I was demonstrating was perceived by others as arrogance, or pushiness, or maybe I unknowingly challenged peoples' thinking by believing everyone just understood and lived by the same awareness I did.

I realize now that my way of being was more "Fire," and then maybe, sometimes, "Ready and Aim," where many people in my circles were more of a "Ready, Ready, Ready," or maybe "Ready, Aim, Aim, Aim" types. As I think back, and as I've asked for honest feedback on who I was being during those times, I've learned that my passion and excitement for the things that inspired me occurred to some as overboard, pushy, and, sometimes even irresponsible. While some people were attracted to my enthusiasm, others saw it as what I now call "firehosing." I knew they were thirsty, so I overwhelmed them with what I thought they needed, when what would have been much more effective was a trickling fountain they could find on their own.

Wanting something more for someone than they want it for themselves only caused me angst. I had to realize that everyone has his/her own journey, including me. Unless I was willing and able to

see people as people with their own stories and experiences, instead of only seeing them as objects getting in my way, I was destined to keep having the same experience over and over (remember message, lesson, problem, crisis?).

Wisdom requires a higher perspective. It requires a deeper understanding of the commonplace.

Wisdom is a quality of mind, a way of looking at life. It is to see life both horizontally and vertically. As you look deeper, you see that all life is connected to everything else and that in turn causes you to take in more—to see wider. Wisdom requires that you arrange what you observe and know and create meaning from it.

You build wisdom when you know your strengths and know where to go to leverage your weaknesses instead of trying to shore them up.

Life is too short to spend your months, weeks, days, hours or even minutes in regret. Get over the notion that there is a shortcut to success. There will be pain; but make sure, at the end of the day, it's the pain of hard work and not the pain of regret.

When it's really impactful, wisdom comes back around. Here's a meme that's been circling the internet:

- 1000 BC: Here, eat this root.
- AD 1000: That root is heathen. Say this prayer.
- AD 1800: That prayer is pure superstition. Here, take this potion.
- AD 1940: That potion is snake oil. Here, take this pill.

- AD 1980: That pill is ineffective. Here, take this antibiotic.
- AD 2000: That antibiotic doesn't work. Here, eat this root.

How will you stop this endless cycle? JUST STOP! Think something original - or at least original for you. It may not be the first time someone thought of it, but that's where collective wisdom comes from! Find others to talk with about your ideas. But don't just look for people who agree with your perspective. You will never grow if everyone thinks exactly the same way.

Go to any bookstore and you will find a huge section called Self Help. (Note that there is no section called "Group Help." We don't have a genre for connecting and learning and growing together – yet!) In that Self Help section there are countless books claiming to give you a "tried and true" or a "guaranteed to give you results" or a "follow this and you're sure to succeed" promise that will change your life. Why does that surefire answer approach just not sit well with me?

Maybe it goes back to my need to find ***the*** answer to all the challenges I wasn't even able to articulate in my own life. I've always been a seeker, an eager learner and an overachiever, so I was a sucker for anything that would promise me results - especially those I could obtain outside myself.

I named my first blog back in 2004 "You Already Know This Stuff"; that may be why I'm still a bit unsettled

by having someone else tell me what I should do or guarantee me results based on their formula for success.

I get that there are certainly great ideas that others have learned from their own experience and that they want to share with others. I'm the same way. I'd love nothing more than to be able to share all the things I continue to learn about my own life so that others might be able to subvert those experiences themselves and get to more important work more quickly.

But for some reason I have a problem with some guru promising others ***the*** way to success.

Maybe it starts with defining that inner KNOWING - the collection of all the wisdom we've accumulated over the years and either discounted because it didn't fit with who we are or accepted because it did. I wonder if we get to a point in our lives that we've accumulated enough inner wisdom - a critical mass, maybe - that makes it easier to trust both ***WHAT*** we know and ***THAT*** we know.

Of course, discernment is a crucial skill that wisdom allows. Discernment is knowing when to handle a situation yourself with all your knowledge and inspiration, and also knowing when to call in the experts. You may be too close to the situation to be objective. Or maybe the situation you are dealing with requires an expert – someone with a specific skillset you don't have who can provide clarity. Sure, you probably could learn how to fix your sink or even how to perform an appendectomy by watching a YouTube video, but would that be the wisest idea?

We can't promise that someone's life will be altered by reading this or any self-help book out there. But we do know that there comes a point in everyone's life - Lance Secretan, in the book *Inspire: What Great Leaders Do,* says that sometimes it happens on people's deathbeds, but it does happen - when they connect with their destiny, when the switch flips and they realize that they can have a life they love.

We sure don't want to wait until we are on our deathbeds, and both of us are learning every day - every minute. Yes, as the Beatles tell us, "Living is easy with eyes closed, misunderstanding all you see/ It's getting hard to be someone but it all works out, it doesn't matter much to me" (from Strawberry Fields Forever).

Don't let fear of the unknown keep you from living with eyes open, learning to understand all you see. It's a much more enlightening place to live as you figure out your own, personalized approach to life!

1 https://www.forbes.com/sites/rodgerdeanduncan/2018/11/07/in-your-world-is-there-wisdom-work/#59d41e026332

TOOLS FOR DEVELOPING WISDOM

Conversational Tools:

In response to a statement like: "We've never/always done that before."
What about this new idea concerns you? Giving something up or the unknown? Are you willing to try?

In response to a complaint:

I get that. I'm glad you brought this up. Do you see anything in this current situation that resembles something you've experienced before? What did you learn there that would be helpful here?

In response to a suggestion:
That is a very interesting idea. Tell me more. Where did you learn about that? In your vision, how did it work and apply to our situation?

In response to a compliment:

Thank you! What about that was meaningful to you?

Experiential Tools:

The results these tools produce will be best measured by recording observations in a small notebook or journal. Choose one of the following "assignments" each week and share observations in weekly team meetings or with a MasterMind group.

When Was the First Time? Sit quietly and ponder the first time you made a big mistake at work. Really go there. What happened? What were the circumstances that caused you to make the mistake? Replay the scene in your mind. What did you learn from that experience? What will you do again in spite of the mistake? What will you not do again in spite of a success? Bring this learning to the forefront and remind yourself that you could only have learned this lesson from this situation. Celebrate your learning!

List Your Upsets. Similar to the previous activity, spend some time listing the people and situations that seem to cause you the greatest angst or frustration. Be sure to use initials only or guard your notes closely so they don't get misinterpreted by someone who might find them lying around. For each frustration, identify the message or lesson that person or situation has to deliver to you. As you work through your frustrations, you will begin to notice that the only situations or people who frustrate you are those who have a lesson to deliver to you. Track your progress as you continue to realize how wise you are becoming!

VAK to the Future. Imagine your ideal future, at work or at home. VISUAL: What will you see in your life that will let you know you've achieved your goal? AUDITORY: What will you hear people saying about you? What will you be saying to yourself? KINESTHETIC: How will you feel? Have you ever felt that feeling before? Close your eyes and get in touch with that feeling now. Where in your body do you feel it the most? If the feeling has a color, what is it? If the feeling has a shape, what is it? If the feeling has a temperature, what is it? If the feeling has a texture, how does it feel when you touch it?

Flashlight. You don't have to know everything. You've gotten to this point in your life because you are smart and capable. Imagine that when you were born it was like living in a huge mansion with dozens of rooms of possibility available to you. Over time as you grew up, rooms of that mansion were closed off to you by advice from parents, older relatives, teachers, people in authority. Eventually as an adult today, imagine the mansion you are living in, but with all those doors closed. Now you're living in a tiny little apartment in the middle of the mansion. You don't even remember that you closed the doors. Take your flashlight and peek into the rooms that you thought were closed. Have you looked there? And there? Work this week to open up a couple of doors and remember why you closed them in the first place. What awareness do you have today that allows you to keep the door open, or choose to keep it closed?

Bamboo. Consider that bamboo planted from seed takes five years underground before it breaks through the ground. You wouldn't be criticized for believing that nothing was happening in those five years. But once it breaks through, it grows very quickly and is very renewable. What dream do you have that is germinating underground? Are you committed to keeping it alive? None of the work shows … and then, one day … What is your bamboo?

Speak Into YES/NO. This is a partner exercise. Pick an A and a B. A tells B about something s/he is very passionate about. It could be a hobby, an interest, a family member. B's job is not to care at all about what A is saying. After one minute, switch roles. After both have gone, the next round B is very interested in A's story. After one minute, switch roles. Debrief by explaining how it felt to speak into the "No" listening space and then the "Yes" listening space. What does this exercise tell us about the importance of active listening?

Step out of your comfort zone. We all know that growth only happens on the other side of our comfort zones, so this week do something that challenges you. Think about one thing that scares you and find a way to do it. If you're afraid of public speaking, find a way to give a presentation at work. If you're hesitant to step into a leadership role but know it would be good for you, volunteer at a local non-profit or join a board for some cause that interests you.

Take a class. Audit a college class or take a community education course that interests you. There are many online learning options from YouTube to Udemy to LifeWorks University. Join a MasterMind group or book club, or even go to the library! Learn a new language, take a cooking class, or join an art or theater group. Share what you experience with your team or family.

Take a freak to lunch. Leadership guru Tom Peters has all kinds of great ideas for expanding your wisdom, including spending time with people who think differently than you do. He affectionately calls these people "freaks." He suggests that a great way to learn and expand your own thinking, is to have lunch with them. Frequently. I've read so many Peters books over the years that I can't even remember where this idea came from, but if you want to learn more about Peters and his amazing mind, a quick Google search will turn up many opportunities for you.

ASK. Don't be afraid to ask for help when you need it. Turn to someone you think of as wise and ask for advice. However, even advice offered by someone you wholly trust should be taken with your own discernment. Ultimately, you are the only person who can decide what's right for you to do. As it says in the Bible, Ask and it shall be given to you; Seek and you shall find; Knock and the door shall be opened unto you. It all starts with your willingness to ASK.

Share your wisdom with others. Think about the mentors who helped you along the way, and find ways to play that role for other people who might be able to benefit from what you've learned. If someone asks for advice, do your best to point them in the direction that seems right. Don't let your personal desires cloud your advice.

Compile best practices lists. Do some research in any area you would like to learn more. This could be at the place you work or for an activity you have an interest in learning outside of work. Chances are good that someone somewhere has already done some sort of work in an area you're looking to improve or master. Create your own research project by digging into online resources, but don't be afraid to just contact someone you'd like to learn from. Instead of reinventing the wheel, compile your own list of best practices based on your findings. Through my own experience I can tell you that it is amazing what can happen if you just pick up the phone and contact someone!

Create. One great way to increase wisdom is to get involved with a new hobby like pottery, or magic tricks, or photography, or art. Doing something creative will help diversify and sharpen your mind. Learning something new each day will stretch your mental muscles and enable you to make better decisions.

Misconception check. Discover associates' misconceptions. See if team members can identify what is the correct answer, when given a false fact. It's useful when going over a previous lesson. It encourages everyone to think deeply and wager all the possibilities.

How would _____________ see this? Play a little game with your team (or even on your own) any time you feel a bit stuck when brainstorming. Put together a list of famous people everyone would know real or fictional. (Examples: Oprah, Abraham Lincoln, Peter Pan, Gandhi, etc.). Now imagine how each of those people might approach your problem or dilemma. What wisdom could that person's perspective bring to your challenge?

(Some of these and more great ideas are found at **https://www.wikihow.com/Gain-Wisdom**)

Energy is the **missing link** between your ambitions and your ability to experience **whatever** you truly desire.

Part Four: ENERGY

Keeping Your Battery Charged

Everything you see, taste, touch, smell, and hear - even those thoughts you think - is made up of vibrating energy. Energy, it its truest form, cannot be created or destroyed. It always was, is now, and always will be. It just takes on different forms.

Energy is something you can't touch, but you can sure feel it.

Energy, as it relates to us as humans, is really a pretty simple concept. It's how you show up in your life. It's your attitude, your demeanor, your outlook. It's that old glass half full or half empty story.

And, when you really think about it, energy is the most important personal resource available. It's the missing link between your ambitions and your ability to experience whatever you truly desire.

Energy manifests itself in various ways, **physical, emotional, mental,** and **spiritual** are just four.

Most people would agree that energy manifests itself in various ways. Physical energy, emotional, mental, and spiritual are just four.

Physical energy is what we learned in science class. Going back to your junior high physical science class for a moment, you might remember that everything: your body, your home, your business, everything you can see with your eyes in the physical universe is made up of physical energy. Whether you can see it or not, you trusted your science teacher who told you that slower, denser energy makes up things like tables and rocks, and higher, lighter energy makes up air and wind.

Take water, as an example. In solid form, it's ice. Heat it up and the molecules and atoms move more quickly. It turns into water. Heat it up even more and it turns into really fast-moving energy that looks like steam. As it evaporates, it has the potential energy inside it to turn back into water, and eventually ice.

Think about a time you have walked into a room where people have been fighting or arguing. Without having been there to witness it, you can feel the heaviness. No one even needs to tell you what happened, you just instantly sense it.

This is how energy works in the physical world. We get it. We can understand it logically.

But that's not the only type of energy that affects us as humans.

No scientific equation is more recognizable than $E=mc^2$, and few are simpler. The discoverer of

this formula, Albert Einstein, was one of the most influential physicists of his time, no question. But he was also a deep thinker and philosopher.

One of the fundamental ideas he believed in was posed by a non-scientific question. The first part of that quote is: ***"I think the most important question facing humanity is, 'Is the universe a friendly place?' This is the first and most basic question all people must answer for themselves."*** (See the entire quote at our website, http://www.powertoolsatwork.com/tools)

The energy around that question FEELS a certain way, and scientifically, it's lighter. Heavy dense energy results in stagnant energy flow, which has a tendency to create *dis-ease* and sickness.

You know energy. You can sense it right now. If you are uncertain, ask yourself how you feel. If you feel good, you're in a higher energy state. If you feel bad, it's a lower state.

Everything you perceive in your physical environment is dependent upon its rate of vibration. And you attract to yourself the vibrational match to that.

Nothing has to be a problem or even a challenge. If you really get clear about this concept, everything is an OPPORTUNITY.

I used to think of the tasks that needed to get done around me as obligations. Over time I shifted to seeing them as responsibilities. But when I shifted to seeing them as opportunities, nothing seemed like a HAVE TO. It was much closer much more often to a GET TO.

So, what's the difference between things you get to do, have to do, and want to do? Certainly there are commonalities between those tasks. But isn't it true that mindset has a lot to do with why tasks fall into one of those categories?

You only **HAVE** to do something until you **WANT** to and then you never **HAVE** to again. I suppose at that point you **GET** to do it. Take paying rent, for example. Instead of thinking "I **HAVE** to pay my rent," shift your energy to a thought like "I am so grateful to have a roof over my head and that I make choices that allow me to pay someone for the privilege of living here."

That may seem like a semantic shift only, but ask yourself: Do those situations **FEEL** different to you? If so, you're starting to understand energy.

I met author and speaker Danielle LaPorte at a retreat in northern Minnesota in 2013 before I even knew who she was. Her book *The Desire Map* was just newly released, and she was talking – in a very candid way – about how business has goal setting backwards.

What? I perked right up to hear more of her, um, *colorful* language around this area which was, to me, necessary, but heavy.

She said instead of coming up with to-do lists – even if they are bucket lists – and traditional business plans and all the things we know we have to accomplish and experience outside of ourselves, what if we instead concentrated on getting in touch with the way we wanted to feel after those things were accomplished?

She told us that the reason we ever accomplish any of those external things is because we have an internal feeling we are chasing.

I could grasp that - intellectually. But putting words to feelings? This was new.

Sure, Napoleon Hill has told us that one of the principles of success from *Think and Grow Rich* is to have a burning desire. He even used that word: Desire. De- of and sire - father. Of the Father. Or in another context desire Latin word desiderare, which could mean "demand" or "express" but had a much prettier literal meaning: "to await what the stars will bring." But still. "Feelings" and "work" together in the same context?

LaPorte calls these *Core Desired Feelings* and even gave a list of possibilities as an example in her book.

When I could wrap my brain around putting words to feelings, that shifted everything about the way I had been being around goal setting. Instead of feeling heavy, this entire concept shifted to light for me. And I began to understand how important energy is to living the life of my dreams.

If something as obvious as goal setting could inspire a feeling, what else could do that?

Energetic awareness is not a term I would have used growing up. There were my five physical senses, and they gave me whatever information I needed to have. Anything beyond that was from the devil. Fear was my motivator for everything from grades to sports success to religion. I was always on the edge of guilt,

knowing that as soon as I said or did something wrong, I'd be in trouble somehow.

Not the most fun way to live.

Nothing seemed to go right when I was in the mindset of beating myself up. I was never good enough at the things I thought would get me recognition and appreciation - I had taken piano lessons for 12 years, and thought I could be an accompanist. But I just wasn't good enough. I didn't love the piano; I wasn't cut out for it. So, I tried out for Pop Singers. But as a tall basketball player, I didn't look good in the dress the smaller girls wore. I didn't make the cut. I decided I wanted to play in the jazz band, but clarinets didn't qualify. I borrowed a classmate's saxophone and learned to play it. But I still didn't make the cut. I guess I just wasn't good enough.

There was an award created to honor a businessman in my hometown, Red Lilyquist, who loved sports and loved kids. I wanted that award, not just because it was given to the senior who showed sports acumen as well as academic achievement, but because Red lived two houses away from me. I'd grown up with him as a neighbor. Well, despite my good grades and my sports excellence, I didn't get it. And it was yet another reinforcement to me that I just couldn't force myself to be accepted. And didn't know why. Nothing seemed to work out.

I didn't realize at the time that I had something to do with the things that showed up in my life. All the things that seemed to go "wrong" were simply information being presented to me to show me what I should be doing instead. I wasn't a "fit in with the crowd" type of gal, yet that's all I knew how to do. I never really found my stride – until I could connect with people on a deeper level. I was working as a life coach before I knew what that meant. And it was never about sharing my story, it was helping them tell theirs.

I was a great listener, and no one really knew me.

I was being something, and not realizing it was my energy that was changing others: allowing them to be who they really were without judgment, even though I was judging myself in the process.

Looking back now, it was practicing ***BEING***. I just ***WAS***. I wasn't trying to do something, I was just being that energy. And that ***BEING*** energy invited others into that space.

Of course, I didn't know any of this consciously. So I would become frustrated and upset with myself for not ***BEING*** what I considered to be good enough. I wasn't attracting others to ask about me, so no one ever really did. I thought I needed their permission and their invitation to be able to share about myself, and because my energy was all about asking them about them, there was no need to share about me.

I was lonely and isolated amid crowds of people.

But that was the path of awareness and understanding that has allowed me to step into my being now.

Frustration and upset have energy. Joy and passion also have energy. Can you imagine the difference?

Catabolic, Anabolic, Pink & Blue

Scientists call this difference catabolic and anabolic energy. Catabolic refers to molecular breakdown, while anabolic refers to the construction of molecules.

This isn't just a scientific concept. Think about it at work. If you have anabolic energy, you are constructive. You're looking for ways to build people and systems up. Catabolic energy at work tends to be destructive. Things need to be fixed.

If you're more on the catabolic side and your salespeople don't hit their goals, you might think nothing of calling them out publicly at a sales meeting. It wouldn't even occur to you that this might impact the culture of your office. Fear and negativity affect everyone, and the people in your office may be afraid to ask for help. Some people thrive in this environment, many don't. Problem solving becomes the focus, and when you solve one problem, you need to find (or create) another so you can accomplish the next goal. Your catabolic energy spreads, and people start following your example in their own circles, both at work and outside of work.

On the other hand, if you lead with anabolic energy, you are always looking to build up and support your employees and associates. If they don't hit their sales goals, you dig deeper to discover what's missing. It might be additional training or increased incentives. With anabolic energy as your way of being, you tend to create a culture of excitement, engagement and loyalty.

In most successful business environments, then, there is a mixture of catabolic and anabolic energy. There is destruction – as when an old system needs to be destroyed to make room for the new construction. In order for creativity to emerge, something old needs to be destroyed. When you create a painting, you need to destroy the blank canvas. When you create a piece of music, you need to destroy the silence.

In a similar fashion, humans are composed of both masculine and feminine energy. There is something about your human experience that will identify more with one or the other in your lifetime, but the balance of the universe has to do with an equal honoring of both.

Over time our civilization has traditionally overemphasized the masculine worldview. The masculine mind is focused on externals. In Western civilization we focus a lot on the tangible: whether or not I can put my hands on it, whether or not I can register it with my physical senses.

When the masculine energy thinks of changing, it works to change something that already exists. It thinks in terms of taking something you don't like and substituting something you do like. On the other hand, it is a feminine function to *create* what you do want. Creating is when you bring *some*thing out of *no*-thing.

Masculine energy is dynamic. It ***DOES***. Feminine consciousness is not dynamic, but magnetic. It is more about ***BEING***.

We've been taught that in order to be "successful" we need to DO something - we need to CHANGE something, we need to show **results**. It's what we can **see** and **touch** that matters. We really believe that touchy feely stuff won't bring about any changes because we can't **see** or **measure** the results.

But we need to go within in order to create the world anew. If we truly want things to be different in our work lives and, really, in our whole lives, we need to think about ***creating***, not ***making***. How is it working in our lives to MAKE somebody DO something? What if we stopped trying to change everyone else and went inside and thought about TRANSFORMING ourselves? When we focus on ourselves, instead of being selfish, we actually do what the flight attendants have been telling us forever: we take care of ourselves first so we are able to be the people others would want to follow.

Certainly, there is always some combination of the masculine and the feminine, of the dynamic and magnetic - and in fact, isn't that the goal: to achieve some sort of harmony?

Let's look at this masculine and feminine energy in a slightly different way. Instead of being so gender specific, what if we considered the relational aspects of work and the transactional ones? The book *Pitch Like a Girl* introduces a really unique way to distinguish this type of energy.

While the premise of Ronna Lichtenberg's book is gender specific, and in it she gives practical tips and exercises to help women get better at pitching their ideas, there is much more information and inspiration to be gotten by thinking outside that strict categorization.

We were most intrigued with Chapter 1: Pink and Blue. At the risk of sounding sexist, and before we get into the distinctions she points out, we want to make it clear that there is no judgment in this distinction. We know many men who we would classify as Pinks (and who would gladly agree with me) and equally as many women who would agree they are more Blue. So this is not a gender issue.

As it relates to energy, we see this as a Relational (Pink) and a Transactional (Blue) focus. In her book Lichtenberg says that "a person with a pink style is someone who wants to connect with you before doing business with you. A 'Pink' will first mention … something, anything, before getting down to the business at hand."[1]

She goes on to say "now Blues, on the other hand, are the opposite of Pinks. They place a high priority on what I call task – just getting the job done. Someone with a blue style just isn't naturally a 'people person' or wants to keep his or her emotional connections outside the office."[2]

If any organization is strictly pink or strictly blue, of course they won't be as effective as they could be. It's the awareness of the distinction, and the willingness to come together and celebrate the distinctions that produces the most harmonious environment.

Love and Fear

Still another way to consider energy is on the Love and Fear scale.

If there were only two ways to look at the experience of living, through one of those two filters, how would that affect your experience of life?

Both are energy.

Several years ago there was a news feature on a morning news program where a surgeon was sharing a new lasik eye surgery, and was conducting the surgery live on a morning TV news show.

The patient was a woman who had worn glasses since she was seven, and had no recollection of life before glasses or contacts. As someone who first got glasses in third grade myself, I could relate.

The real beauty in the news story came when the doctor revealed that this woman, before the surgery, had vision of 20/10,000 - which means that at 20 feet she could see what people with 20/20 vision can see at 10,000 feet. She is legally blind and had lived in fear that she may lose a contact while she was driving, or misplace her glasses and not be able to care for her children in an emergency.

The doctor explained that people with vision as poor as this woman's are the most frightened of having the surgery because they know what it is like to be blind and their fear of losing what little sight they do have often prevents them from having the surgery.

The doctor's demeanor and delight were refreshing as he talked about how blessed he felt to be able to give the gift of sight to people like this woman. After the procedure when the woman was able to see for the first time without corrective lenses, she was thanking him profusely with tears running down her cheeks. His response: "You're the one who was brave enough to have the procedure done. You made the leap - I was just here to catch you."

How often do we stand on the brink, unwilling or unable to make the leap because we're not 100% certain the net will appear? Maybe we have it in our head that that net needs to look a certain way before we will jump. If we're worried about all the things that might happen if we leap and the net doesn't appear - or it won't be the right color - or it might not be strong enough - or a whole host of other "what ifs," we're giving up the opportunity for something even better.

In the case of this woman, the net appeared as a loving pair of arms.

If fear is your predominant way of seeing the world – what Einstein defined as an unfriendly attitude and scientific terminology might call catabolic energy – would it be any surprise that that's what keeps showing up?

Theoretically and hypothetically, this probably makes sense. But leaping out into the world means TAKING ACTION. Love supports that action; fear supports staying the same.

No Such Thing As Status Quo

Is there really such a thing as "staying the same?" After all, isn't that really what status quo implies? If you're at all familiar with nature, you realize that no two days are exactly alike. And since, as early 20th century author and philosopher Wallace D. Wattles reminds us in his book *The Science of Getting Rich*, "there is a thinking stuff from which all things are made and which, in its original state, permeates, penetrates, and fills the interspaces of the universe,"[3] we are all connected with all that is anyway.

So, if there is no static status quo, it would stand to reason that there are only two ways the thinking stuff of the universe can take us: toward creation or toward disintegration.

If we are always either creating or destroying, and we are aware of this, why wouldn't we intend creation?

If we're doing nothing, we are disintegrating. Dis: "do the opposite of" and Integrate: "to unite or combine." So, disintegrate really means to break apart; to lose integrity. Gravity works against us if we are doing nothing. But science also tells us that bodies in motion have an effect on other bodies in motion. As long as we are in motion, we will be in creation mode.

Now all movement is not growth. Sometimes, in order to distract ourselves from what is really important, we get busy. We find ourselves in motion, sure, but is that motion toward or away from our intended result?

Consider the activity that happens during a game of pool. It's possible to just take a stab at the cue ball and let it go flying across the table without aiming at anything in particular. The ball will move and may very well encounter other balls, sending them into motion as well, but it is not likely that a desired shot will just happen randomly.

When you take the time to line up your shot, find the best angle, and only exert the amount of energy necessary to get the ball to strike your desired target, the odds are much greater that you will achieve your goal. It's not that the ball in the first example wasn't in motion; it's just that it wasn't in effective motion.

Thoughtful, measured energy applied toward the desired outcome will be much more successful in helping achieve whatever you are attempting.

Since we're learning there is no such thing as status quo, if we do nothing, we are still moving; just at a much slower pace. And the direction is due to gravity, which is down, toward density. All objects are in motion, but the slower the motion, the denser the object.

Wouldn't it stand to reason that the same would be true for our physical energy? The faster we move physically, the lighter we become. What about our thinking? The more energized and enlivening our thoughts, the lighter (more light-filled) we become. We use the term "dark" to imply when things are off (after all, have you ever heard of a "dark switch?" When you want to fill a room with light, you turn on

the "light switch."). And the term "light" has several connotations which imply things like bright and not heavy.

Given a choice (which we ***always*** have), why not choose light and creation?

Now apply this to your home, work, or school life. If we are "staying the same," we are actually disintegrating - breaking apart, losing integrity. We tell ourselves we want to maintain the "status quo," but the world around us is changing, growing, moving, learning, creating. If we say we want to take a year off, just chill and maintain, at the end of that year we will actually be 365 days behind because we were not intentionally creating.

Our minds cannot maintain positive and negative thoughts at the same time; one has to take precedence. And if we're not putting in the positive consciously, the space will fill with the negative or denser energy.

So, one way to maintain the energy and the motion is to get around other objects that are in motion. After all, objects in motion will remain in motion when they are influenced by other objects in motion.

Like-minded and like-hearted people are the same way. They are intentionally creating their outcomes and their futures. And they will remain in creation mode when they are around others who are also in creation mode.

Seven Levels of Energy

Author and founder of the Institute for Professional Excellence in Coaching (iPEC) Bruce D. Schneider has developed an energy leadership index which gives another context to catabolic and anabolic energy. In the coaching world, Schneider's work identifies Anabolic energy as the positive energy in a person's life, and Catabolic as the destructive energy in a person's life.

Awareness is key to understanding your own energy, and then demonstrating that awareness at work and in all aspects of life, in order to work toward positive change.

Jodi Grinwald is a master practitioner of the Energy Leadership Index and at a 2017 presentation at Berkeley College, she shared her analysis of the seven levels. Following is a summary of her report.

Level 1

Core emotions: Guilt, self-doubt, hopelessness, fear, worry, depression

These leaders are critically self-aware but fail to take action. Level one leaders typically have low self-esteem, work in crisis mode and lack productivity.

"Some leaders have little to no passion or commitment to their company's mission," said Grinwald. "They may not remember it because they are (usually) reacting to crises, and they don't have a real plan for where they are going. Their communication skills are poor to nonexistent, as is their ability to truly inspire and motivate others."

Level 2

Core emotions: anger, resentment, hatred, blame, greed, discord, pride

For these leaders, actions and results come from a place of anger and defiance. The focus is on others, stress, disappointment, resistance, struggle, control and entitlement.

Often interactions with these types of leaders feel like a zero-sum game, in which their world is made up of winners (them) and losers (everyone else). It's not uncommon for Level 2 leaders to be micromanagers.

Level 3

Core emotions: relief, peace of mind

It is at this level that there is a distinctive shift between fear (Level 1) and negative energy (Level 2) to positive energy and a willingness to accept responsibility for one's actions.

Level 3's thoughts are positive, and their emotions come from a place of forgiveness. Actions and results may include rationalization, justification, tolerance and coping.

Level 4

Core emotions: compassion, love, gratitude

This leader's focus is on their team. They genuinely care about others, and they don't take anything personally. Instead, they are able to view circumstances and people objectively. They are playful, generous, supporting, helpful and self-caring.

Grinwald noted that this kind of leader performs best in human resources, customer service and sales because of their exceptional people skills.

Level 5

Core emotion: peace

Leaders who operate at a Level 5 live to the fullest and don't let the past get in the way. They are open-minded and focus on the organization as a whole rather than just themselves.

Often, when faced with a challenge or threat, these leaders view them as an opportunity for growth and development. Further, these individuals don't try to change differences in others, but instead focus on accepting and reconciling differences.

Level 6

Core emotion: joy

These leaders are driven by their intuition, and they are often creative geniuses and visionaries. Individuals at this level of leadership see others around them as an extension of themselves, which fosters an attitude of empowerment and achievement among team members.

"With Level 6 leaders, everyone always wins," said Grinwald. "These leaders are brilliant and conscious leaders."

Level 7

Core emotion: passion

The seventh and highest level is often the hardest to achieve, and few people have ever experienced it. It's characterized by a complete lack of blame, shaming and fear of failure.

Ultimately, said Grinwald, when you are more aware of your leadership style and the impact it has on your employees and co-workers, you can study the other leadership styles and work toward being the type of leader you want to be.[4]

More information about Schneider's Energy Leadership Index can be found at our website.

Choose Your Words Carefully

The words you choose to use, either in your speech or even just what you tell yourself in your thinking process, is the way you see the world. The way you connect.

Language is the most effective way to convey information, so it's crucial that you are aware of the energy the words you choose carry.

What do you tell yourself? If you are not putting energy into your thoughts on purpose, you are destined to take that context from your conditioning. When you have the awareness, you can ask for guidance and be on purpose.

We give up so many **opportunities to be happy** by holding on to that **ingrained need to be right.**

What is your I AM language? Is it negative or what's wrong (catabolic) or is it affirming and building you up (anabolic)?

The language you choose has its own energy. Because of our emotional attachment to certain words, they actually create our lives. Our words color, and also expose, how we view our world.

Don't be afraid to just ***BE*** every now and then. Think about your mind like a snow globe ... when it's shaken up and frantic and frenzied, it just needs to settle down every once in a while. Then you can enjoy the scene inside the snow globe. Take it from someone who lives in North Dakota: it's not as easy to see the scene when it's snowing!

That's energy. We want to be around those who support us and who give off positive vibes as we struggle to maintain the small flicker of new energy that we create when we get outside our own boxes and sometimes fall back into that familiar place of self-fulfilling prophesy ("It'll never work anyway" and then we get to be right about it).

We give up so many opportunities to be happy by holding on to that ingrained need to be right.

It's All Made Up

As someone who works from home, I sometimes need a change of pace, so often do work at various coffee shops. One afternoon as I was working, the man behind the counter came over to where I was sitting because the TV was on above my head. He shared his worry because the Dow was going down. He wanted to engage me in that conversation by asking whether I thought it was because the Fed is waiting for the government to do something or other (or maybe it was the other way around).

To be honest with you, and with him, I'm just not that involved in the Dow or the rising gas prices or the weather or other things I really have no direct control over in this moment.

When I told him that in just a few words, he asked whether or not I had money in the stock market. I told him that I did, but that I have someone else worrying about that for me. He looked at me as if I'd just grown another head.

Am I crazy?

I decided a few years ago that the energy I wasted worrying about those things I can't control was taking its toll on my effectiveness and creativity and I gave it up. I also gave up guilt at that time and began concentrating my energy and efforts not on the past or even in the future, but became much more present. What I realized during the coffee shop encounter was that while I may

lose money in the stock market, I gain some peace and clarity - a LOT of peace and clarity, in fact.

If I'm worried now about something that has happened with my money which I'm not going to need until some future time when the value will be completely different anyway, it seems to me that I'm giving up my opportunity to be happy right now by worrying about it.

This was a great reminder to me that I really have been happier in the past couple of years - and have been even more effective in my business and my relationships.

So, what do we say to the people who call us irresponsible or out of touch or idealistic? Maybe it's not what we ***SAY***, but how we ***BE***. Actions speak louder than words, after all.

Responding or Reacting?

As mentioned earlier, the tools we are offering here are responses, not reactions. One of the differentiators may be how the stimulus is interpreted (that which causes either pleasure or pain). Is it out of a response or a reaction? To do either involves choice. Reacting means we have given that choice to someone or something outside of ourselves.

We find ourselves in reaction mode when we do not have time to create the future because we are so busy handling the present. Heck, in reaction mode, the future can only look a lot like the present because it doesn't require any original thought on our part. It's based on our emotions, not our thinking.

When we respond, we take back control. We anticipate things to come and think about them before saying or doing anything. We get to decide how, and really if, we allow outside forces to affect us, both externally and internally. When we respond instead of react, we actually feel more at ease (or less in dis-ease) and actually have many more opportunities to move toward pleasure instead of away from pain.

Despite the fact that nearly all of us are ***able*** to respond to things instead of react to them (that's why it's assumed that when we get to a certain age, we are response-able), it appears that not all of us are ***willing*** to do so.

One way to determine whether you are spending more time reacting or responding is to check your results. What's happening in your life? Are you happy, fulfilled, energized, surrounded by great people, feeling pretty fortunate? Or more the opposite - like a victim of your surroundings and upbringing? In other words, when you do make a move in your life, is it away from things or toward them?

Shaking a fist (or a certain finger) at a driver in a parallel lane on the highway or sharing a less-than-positive comment about a friend, relative, or even a grumpy server at a restaurant just seems a little pointless.

A question to ask before taking those kinds of actions is: "What good will it do?"

That is really a very objective question. However, the intention and inflection will determine the outcome. Using a defeatist attitude is distinct from focusing on the good that can be infused by actions from that perspective. (See more about this question in the Tools section at the end of this chapter.)

We believe in the goodness of people - and we believe that all people have huge capacity for goodness. But when good people do nothing - are not moved to action to demonstrate their goodness – that's when we remain at the mercy of the loudest voice. And the loudest voice doesn't have to be loud in volume - it can be the loudest voice because it's the only one doing the declaring.

If we're not able to take a stand FOR what we believe in - expanded capacity, love-based workplaces, world peace - we end up by default represented by what our thoughts may be telling us we DON'T want ... but what our silence has provided for us.

That which commands the most attention "wins," not by force, but sometimes by momentum and habit and inactivity. Just think how much more we can ***DO*** and ***BE*** when we don't have to ***DO*** and ***BE*** it alone.

The energy that you put out into the world comes back to you many times over, and being conscious of that energy, do you like what's coming back?

Just stop at some point today and think about exactly what you're thinking and what you're doing. Ask yourself, before you react, "what ***GOOD*** will it do?" and then make your choice.

We're confident you'll see things you never knew you never knew.

1 Ronna Lichtenberg, *Pitch Like A Girl*, (New York: Rodale, 2005) p. 14.
2 Ibid p. 15
3 Wallace D. Wattles, *The Science of Getting Rich*, public domain.
4 https://www.businessnewsdaily.com/10517-energy-leadership-levels.html

TOOLS for BUILDING ENERGY

Conversational Tools:

In response to a statement like: "I don't have enough time" or "It just doesn't feel right."
Tell me more about that. Does thinking about what you have to do cause you to feel heavy or light?

In response to a complaint:
Acknowledge the complaint using a "feel" word.
How would you like to feel instead? (Here are some examples if they have trouble putting words to feelings)

Acknowledged
Alive
Amazing
Bold
Bright
Calm
Centered
Certain
Courageous
Creative
Decisive
Determined
Energized
Excited
Free
Grounded
Happy
Inspired
Joyful
Optimistic
Positive
Quiet
Relaxed
Secure
Supported
Touched
Valued
Vivacious
Vital

In response to a suggestion:
I hadn't thought about that. That's interesting. Tell me more. (How does their suggestion cause you to feel? If heavy, acknowledge it for you. If light, tell them that.)

In response to a compliment:
(Feel it! Take it in! Be genuine in whatever your response.)

Experiential Tools:

The results these tools produce will be best measured by recording observations in a small notebook or journal. Choose one of the following "assignments" each week and share observations in weekly team meetings or with a MasterMind group.

Keep a Victory Journal. You won't remember the specifics of the small wins you experience daily unless you record them. Don't wait to only celebrate the big victories; as you notice what causes you to feel joyful and appreciated and any other feeling you desire, you will begin to trace your feeling back to an action. The more you recognize the connection, the more you can reproduce those desired outcomes.

Love Over Fear. Imagine that every day before you get out of bed, you get to choose whether you put on the glasses of fear or the glasses of love. How you choose to see the world is how you will see it. If you choose fear, you will begin to question and doubt even

the most sincere peoples' motives. Your vision will become clouded with cynicism and resignation. But if you choose love, you will see that even fear has a purpose. It's to keep you safe. It's not about getting rid of fear from your vocabulary, it's seeing it for what it is: a signal. You will recognize how you give up your own ulterior motives and how you begin to listen without judgment. Make it a game to see the world in a whole new way and over time it will appear that way to you automatically.

Burning Desire. Start by imagining a "wouldn't it be nice if ..." scenario. This can be in your work environment or at home or anywhere else you want to play. Let yourself determine whether that is a "nice to have" or a "I can't live without" experience or item.

Put Yourself in Time Out. Communication is never effective when one or both sides of a discussion are angry. So if you feel your blood pressure going up, take a time-out.

A time-out can happen on an informal level, where you essentially just take a break from a charged situation. Typically, a time-out is done on a physical level, where you actually go somewhere else, like into another room or outside. Think about where you could physically go before you get into an angry or highly charged situation because it's more difficult to think clearly then.

Tell someone your plan and let them know how long you will be gone. When you come back, you will either feel better or not. If you're not yet ready to re-engage, tell the person.

Box Breathing. When you are feeling especially stressed but can't put yourself in Time Out, try Box Breathing. Draw a box with your finger on your desk or even in the air as you follow the instructions. Breathe in through your nose filling up your belly for 4 seconds (trace one side of the box). Hold for 4 seconds (trace the next side). Exhale through your mouth for 4 seconds (trace the third side). Hold for 4 seconds (trace the fourth side). Repeat x 4

It is called box breathing because that's an easy way to visualize this breathing technique. You are essentially breathing in a box shape by figuring each of the four seconds as one side of the box. After each round, you should have completed one box breath. Your body cannot be physically stressed while you are box breathing, so after four rounds you should feel more in control.

Be Curious, Not Furious. Instead of allowing your emotions and your frustrations to get the better of you, remind yourself to get Curious, not Furious. Notice what Furious feels like and take inventory of whatever it was that caused you to feel that way. Ask yourself the question "What good will it do?" five times, each

time stressing a different word. 1. **WHAT** good will it do? 2. What **GOOD** will it do? 3. What good **WILL** it do? 4. What good will **IT** do? 5. What good will it **DO**? Simply allowing yourself to be curious about the various inflections and how they alter the feeling of the question will give you some time to control your energy.

Use the question "What difference will it make?" in a similar fashion to shift perspective.

Ducks in a Row. We all know what it means to get our ducks in a row. We wait until everything is perfectly lined up before we do anything. Take a lesson from Mama Duck: She doesn't wait until the babies are lined up to take off. She takes off and the babies line up behind her. If it helps, get a few rubber duckies and line them up on your desk. It will remind you and others to take action despite not having everything perfectly lined up.

Another way to use the ducks is to notice the voice in your head. You know the one that is always telling you what to do, what not to do, you're not good enough, blah, blah, blah, quack, quack, quack. It's like a duck going crazy in your head. Well, sometimes you just need to shut the duck up!

Assume Positive Intent. Those three little words can make a huge difference when you are dealing with other people. Even when they cause you angst

and upset, keep in mind that it's up to you to assume positive intent: that they are really doing the best they can with what they know. Even if they aren't, your energy will stay high because you're doing your part to keep it there.

Hell Yes. This is a simple but powerful decision-making tool. If you need to make a decision and your gut response isn't HELL YES! then it's a no. And no is a complete sentence.

Another way to think of this is to use a really tried and true decision-making tool: flipping a coin. Narrow your choices down to two – heads and tails – and flip the coin. If as soon as the coin leaves your finger you find yourself hoping for one side or the other, you already know the answer. Don't wait for two out of three!

Nut on a String. Get yourself a small hex nut or metal washer and loop a string through it. Draw an 8" diameter circle on a piece of paper and draw a cross through the middle of the circle, dividing it into 4 wedges. Number the wedges 1, 2, 3, and 4. Suspend the nut over the crosshair on the diagram. Make sure it is completely still. Now think of a number in your mind and watch the pendulum swing to that number. You can think "clockwise," "counterclockwise," or any other number or sequence you want. See how powerful your energy is?

Sport Bitching. When all else fails, hold a good old-fashioned bitch session about whatever is bugging you the most. Go into the bathroom or in a closet or someplace no one will witness your ritual and get it all out. Go ahead. Kick. Stomp. Cry. In fact, you can do this anytime at any place if you do it in your mind. Take any item on your problem list – it can be a true obstacle or a silly little upset. Sit down and really contemplate why this is such a problem. Take out a sheet of paper and write "It Can't Be Done" on the top. Now go ahead and be whiny. Write down everything that will never work and every reason you don't deserve what you want and whatever occurs to you.

Now take a look at your list and have some fun with it. Be melodramatic. Exaggerate. Swear, if you have to. Say anything in your mind as long as it's a mean, miserable complaint with some punch to it.

Did you notice that your energy level went up? Does your goal suddenly look a little less impossible? You haven't solved anything yet. The problem is still there. Your doubts are still there. So why are you laughing? Because you've dug down through all those heavy layers of "I can't" and struck a defiant gusher of "I don't want to and I won't." Negativity is energy – pure, ornery, high-octane energy. It's just been so repressed and tabooed that we've forgotten something every 2-year-old knows: how good it is for us to throw a

WARNING:

For the next five minutes I'm in

Sport Bitching

mode – I'm bitching for the sport of it.

The key is to be done and get on with whatever needs to get done.

tantrum. Inside every one of us is an obnoxious, exuberant little brat just squirming to be let out.

Trying to force a positive attitude is the surest way in the world not to get something done. A negative attitude, on the other hand, will get you to do it.

You know you have to do things you don't like to do. So admit it. Hate it. Kick it around the room. Swear at it. And when you're all through, put it back on the table and do it.

Of course, you don't want to take others down with you when you're having your pity party. If others are around or happen to overhear you, just tell them what you're doing. "For the next five minutes I'm in Sport Bitching mode – I'm bitching for the sport of it." And then go to town. Others might even join you. The key is to be done and get on with whatever needs to get done. Bitching for the sport of it gets old really fast – for you, the participant, and for your audience. (Ideas from *Wishcraft* by Barbara Sher)

Shake it Off. When you really need to release some energy, crank up the Taylor Swift, jump up and SHAKE IT OFF! Shake your hands and dance along with Taylor. Really do this and you will feel so much better! Whether it's ridding yourself of negative vibes or pumping yourself up before a presentation at work, this song does wonders!

Taking responsibility really offers the most freedom you could ever want at work and in your personal life.

Part Five: RESPONSIBILITY

If It Is To Be, It Is Up To Me

Ask yourself: "What keeps happening to me?"

Take out a piece of paper and write down a list.

Got the list done? How did that feel? Heavy? That's because victim energy looks at everything that happens as a personal attack at worst, and bad luck at best.

Now take that piece of paper and crumple it up. Slam dunk it into the trash. Let's start again.

Instead, ask yourself: "What keeps happening FOR me?"

Similar question, very different energy. And a very different focus.

To what or to whom am I most responsible? If the answer is not "myself," why is that? In order to be the most effective as a member of any team, I need to work first on myself.

When you get that it's possible to imperfectly accept responsibility and start acknowledging the way you ask that question, you will start to realize taking responsibility really offers the most freedom you could ever want at work and in your personal life.

And your decision to work on yourself first will be like dropping a pebble into a pond. The ripples start with you, but go outward in concentric circles, eventually impacting all of humanity.

Don't make that heavy ... just drop the pebbles on purpose and watch the ripples.

Responsibility and Accountability

Another term many use to address personal responsibility is accountability, which may be defined in this context as an obligation or willingness to accept responsibility or to account for one's actions.

Personal accountability expert and author of the book *QBQ: The Question Behind the Question* John G. Miller teaches that accountability is not something to hold others to: it starts with me. He says that personal accountability can affect others when leaders learn to ask different questions that eliminate victim thinking, blame, and procrastination from their own lives first.

Author and consultant Peter Block inspires much of our work and our thinking. We discovered him as we were reading his book *The Answer to How is Yes* in an early MasterMind study group years ago. His work has continued to inform both our positions on leadership and impact.

According to his website, Peter is an author, consultant and citizen of Cincinnati, Ohio, where he proudly stands for transformation within that community. His work is about empowerment, stewardship, chosen accountability, and the reconciliation of community.

Block co-authored a book called *Freedom and Accountability at Work* where he identified the main cause of blame.

"A root cause of the blame, judgment, and complaining is our denial of our freedom. We institutionally deny the fact that each of us - through our actions and our view of the world - is creating the organization and the leadership we are so fond of complaining about. Deciding that I have created the world around me - and therefore I am the one to fix it - is the ultimate act of accountability.[1]"

While taking responsibility and being willing to be accountable are actually the highest forms of control you could ever want, when it comes down to it, most people will think it's all about the other person. They think accountability is something they hold others to and they seem to think they can make their organizations better by rewarding, punishing, coercing, forcing, bribing others to hold up their end of whatever bargain they think they're creating before they decide to do it themselves.

Share your opinion with the intent to **create dialogue**, where you suspend assumptions in order to learn. Not to be right and to convince, but from a place of **openness** and a **willingness to understand first** before needing to be understood.

In that light, all that ever happens is coercion – a game of chicken of which no one seems to want to be the loser.

Block uncovers a core belief: "with freedom comes accountability, with accountability comes guilt, and with guilt comes anxiety. Since our freedom leads to anxiety, it is easier to repress it than to bear it proudly."[2]

We adopt a "you owe me" mentality which we call freedom, but fight desperately to be like everyone else.

When any of us realize that we have the choice to take total responsibility for our life's situation, no matter what it is, we may feel guilt, but we also may realize a true sense of power, control, and direction we've never seen in an earlier awareness.

Making excuses has, for many people, become an automatic reaction to negative feelings, and it may appear to be a tough hole from which to dig out of. Yet the only way to get out of the hole is to stop digging and seek a new solution . When you discover yourself to be in the hole, it is helpful to pause and ask yourself "Am I telling myself a story here? If so, what is the story? Are there other ways to see the situation? Am I the cause of my situation because I'm not aware of my part in this?"

If they take the concept of personal responsibility to heart, leaders at work and at home begin to realize that if the student or associate or employee hasn't learned, the teacher hasn't taught. As a true leader who is committed to personal responsibility, then, I begin to realize that I am responsible for teaching you that you are responsible for yourself: your attitude, your mindset, your words, and your actions.

You are never without a plethora of choices in your world. You choose whether to accept and embrace your religion, your boss's leadership, your cultural norms. You choose whether to stick or to switch, which team to root for, and which cause to stand for. As you choose the fight instead of the stand, you begin to realize that it is no accident that what you think about you bring about. Choosing the values you choose also brings to you the consequences of those choices.

If you truly believe that management is responsible for employee actions, both "sides" of this conversation then have permission to blame the other for any disappointment. This might be the true definition of collusion: holding the other to the behavior you say you deplore, but holding onto it because you wouldn't have anything to do if you didn't need to fight that behavior in others.

This is not to say that you can't have a political opinion, a religious affiliation, or be for or against anything you choose. It is about knowing yourself and your values.

You can choose to share your opinion when appropriate, but be sure to do so with the intent to create dialogue, where you suspend assumptions in order to learn. Not to be right and to convince, but from a place of openness and a willingness to understand first before needing to be understood.

Benjamin Zander is the conductor of the Boston Youth Symphony and the co-author, with his wife Roz, of the book and video training program called *The Art of Possibility*. One of Ben's foundational teachings is what he calls "Shining Eyes."

As the leader of the orchestra, Ben knows that he is the only member of the orchestra who doesn't make a sound, yet he is the one whose picture is on the cover of the CD or album. He might appear to be very important, but without the orchestra, he is nothing. He realizes it is his responsibility, as the leader, to look for the shining eyes in his players. He knows that if their eyes aren't shining, he needs to ask himself who he is being that is preventing or keeping those eyes from shining.

Leaders who step into that level of accountability and responsibility see that their main job is much less about what they *do*, but what they allow to come out in the people they lead or impact.

When you step into your own personal responsibility, there may be understandings that sometimes you wish you didn't know. After all, a new understanding about your own impact means that you can't go back to the way things used to be before you knew better.

One of those new understandings will be that you have allowed what happens around you. Don't be upset with what you tolerate, in others and in yourself. If you are upset, there must be another way. Not necessarily *better*, but *different*. The only way to better is through different anyway, so if something is to change, something must change.

Over what does any individual have the most control? Himself or herself. Always and forever.

When we act with accountability and responsibility, we tap into the source of our own power. We don't wait for someone else to fix things ***for*** us, we fix what we can ***in*** us. And we do that because we want to, not because we have to. If we're making changes based on someone else's opinion or someone else's suggestion or command, and they don't resonate with our core, they won't stick.

We have, collectively, bought into the vocal minority – the loudest voice – which says that people need to be led, directed, nurtured, trained, coached, rewarded. That belief has played into the bureaucracy which most will say they hate, yet few seem WILLING to transcend. If we truly wanted to and were committed to eliminating the hierarchy and bureaucracy as we say, it can be done in an instant. Just stop believing it is necessary.

If you are waiting and insisting on strong leadership in order for you to be more effective or efficient, you need to know you can have that in an instant, too. Just provide it. Give to another what you most want for yourself.

When we truly understand the concept of responsibility ***for*** us instead of what happens ***to*** us, we realize the clue is to be unattached and non-judgmental about other people and outside circumstances. We learn that the greatest opportunity for us is to build our observation and compassion muscles.

Taking full responsibility for relationships seems counterintuitive. Because concepts only exist in relationship to something else, it may feel like each side needs to hold up their end of the bargain. That's what we've been conditioned to believe. It's 50/50, right?

As a parent or a supervisor or a leader, you might think you need to hold on tighter and direct more when it's really the opposite.

50/50 or 100/100?

In his book and video program *The 100/0 Principle*, Al Ritter suggests that you take 100% responsibility for everything and expect nothing back in exchange or in return. You provide 100% and expect 0%.

The 100/0 concept is probably a bit foreign to you if you're like most people. We've heard about 50/50 relationships (which, oddly enough, only add up to one whole person in the relationship) and maybe even 100/100, where we hope both will be willing to do their fair share of heavy lifting. But in that case, both feel the weight, and have eyes out for the equal distribution of effort. "I'll do it if you will, but you go first," is often a core belief.

But if relationship is truly about connection, and if the 50/50 or even the 100/100 context is applied, the degree of that connection will be dependent upon how related the individuals are to each other. It's not a matter of degree. It never is in the 100/0 mentality.

This does not mean you have to give everything and expect nothing in return even when people are abusive or demanding. It is perfectly appropriate to love from a distance, to send a silent blessing and move on when you are not a harmonious and vibrational match. This is not a judgment, simply an observation and an exercise of free will and choice.

If you find yourself resisting that notion, it's probably a good idea to be the ***LEARNER***, not the ***KNOWER***. You'll recognize this distinction by some sort of physical clue: clenched fists or jaw, tight shoulders, upset stomach. All are physical clues to your emotional state, and are great signposts on the way to higher awareness.

When you take full responsibility and expect nothing, your relationship must take priority over your expectation.

When you are attached to the specifics and the how instead of committed to the outcome, you will find your frustration and anxiety levels are high. The only reasons you are frustrated come down to one (or more) of these three fundamental ideas:

1) An unfulfilled expectation
2) An undelivered communication
3) A thwarted intention

And you are the common denominator, which means you have all the power to change whatever you don't prefer.

Knowing you ***have*** the power and actually ***grabbing*** and ***using*** that power are two very different things.

You are ultimately responsible for allowing the space for the relationship - not for making someone do something or feel something. Working on ***ME*** means I become the person to whom specific things can't be or can't help but be attracted. It's all about vibrational harmony.

Your ultimate responsibility is to yourself, knowing that the outcome is the effect. When you are sincere and authentic, the Law of Attraction (LOA) is a certainty. (And here's the secret: The LOA makes no judgments. Like the law of gravity, it works every single time in every single circumstance.)

When I was a Team Leader at Keller Williams Realty, we had a process for hiring which created preferred profiles for each position, and then asked candidates to take that assessment to see how they matched up with the ideal candidate.

I was hiring for a position and used that process to vet the candidates. In one instance the candidate seemed to be ideal for the position - in person. She interviewed very well. But as we started talking more about her assessment and the preferred profile, hers was almost completely opposite. It simply wasn't a match. That's not to say that it couldn't have worked, but vibrationally the job called for activities that just didn't fit her personality and after validating the assessment with her, that became glaringly obvious to both of us.

By being honest with each other, we realized that we were saving each of us time, effort, and perhaps even heartache. I allowed her the space to be who she really was - to own her own assessment results - and to trust the process.

Responsibility and Communication

When we talk specifically about the aspects of responsibility over which each of us has the most opportunity for growth and development and, eventually, demonstration, of course communication rises to the top.

As a communication major in college, I took all kinds of classes to teach me how to speak, persuade, interview, and present, but it wasn't until several years after I graduated that I had my first formal training in active listening when I became a crisis hotline volunteer. When all you have is a phone between you and a person with a gun to his head, you better have learned active listening skills.

Yet where do most people who aren't hotline volunteers get active listening training if it's not often (or sometimes ever) taught even in a college communication major?

Your biggest responsibility in a communication exchange is to be fully present in your listening. To suspend your own assumptions for the time you are together and just provide open space for the other person to speak into.

It is crucial to realize that what is heard is often not what is said. And as the listener, it's your responsibility to make sure what you heard is what the speaker meant.

If the voice of the ego speaks first and speaks loudest, how much attention should we really give to the ranting and raving voices? And if the loudest voice wins, is there a need to compete?

Consider the statement "Defense is the first offense." Why would anyone ever feel the need to defend anything, including an opinion? Does my truth really need defending? On the other hand, if the dissenting voice is always going to be the loudest, does that mean that the other voices don't need to be heard?

If you stop feeling the need to defend a position or a candidate or an opinion, will the loudest voice win by default or will the debate go away because one side stops playing? Think of this as it relates especially to religion and politics, two issues that seem to spur a win/lose attitude. What if there was no winner or loser - no right or wrong - no good or bad - there just is what is?

People seem to be realizing that the way they've been doing things just isn't producing the results they'd like in their lives, and they might be ready to take some responsibility for altering their talk to gain different results. Each of us has the opportunity to shift the energy in every conversation and to choose not to participate in negative talk, whether that's on the radio or the internet or with our families and friends.

If we are committed to **the light**, we don't always have to be the **candle** - we can sometimes be the **mirror**.

Both are responsible for **illumination**.

Let's stop the defense and, in turn, stop the offense; really, let's just start waking up to the results in our lives and change our minds about what we really want. Once we know what we want, we can choose to stand for that, rather than fighting against something or someone else.

Several years ago when I first started writing a blog, I met people from around the world who were exploring virtual connections through that somewhat new platform. One of the first blogs I was attracted to was Nick Smith's Life 2.0.

While I've lost track of Nick over the years, I've never forgotten this thought he shared on one of his posts which remains as relevant (if not more so) today:

> *"... maybe the problem is not with our leaders but with us. I don't think it's so much that we've made poor choices in electing our leaders, but that we seem to have developed a greater willingness to project the blame for our ills on others, so as to relieve ourselves of our own responsibility. It's as though 'blame' is the purpose we subconsciously want to give to our leaders, and that is the one they are fulfilling for us.... and perfectly so."*

I believe what was causing the distress and *dis-ease* we were witnessing then and remains as applicable now can be culled down to fear, as we talked about earlier in the Energy section of this book.

The first step to eliminating fear is to shed light on and acknowledge 1) that that's what it is and 2) that we actually do feel it. When I was a little kid, dark rooms were very frightening because my imagination made up all kinds of stories about what could be lurking in the corner or under the bed. But as soon as I turned on the light in the room, the fear went away. Light shines away darkness - or, as Nick points out in his original post, *"forest fires start from just one match, and all the darkness in the world cannot put out the light from just one small flame."*

What is our responsibility in those situations that most frustrate or upset us? We can stay stuck in our own rightness, or we can get out of the right, and bring the light.

Edith Wharton told us that there are two ways of spreading light: to be the candle or the mirror that reflects it. If we are truly committed to the light, does it matter which we choose to be? Both are responsible for illumination.

When we remember that there really is no "out there" "out there," and there is no "us" or "them," only "we," it is much easier to bring our own light to the government, to education, to religion, and to business and commerce whenever we notice. When that attention begins to shift from what is "wrong" or "right" to "what works" or "what doesn't," the energy automatically shifts from judgment to observation. Our own individual, seemingly inadequate or insufficient attitudes or thoughts now become our commitment to be the change we wish to see in the world.

Deepak Chopra once said that leaders are elected or appointed by the collective consciousness of those they represent. If that is true, then we really have no one to "blame," but have an outstanding opportunity for dialogue: suspending assumptions for the purpose of learning something.

That's like flipping the switch: helping shift the focus and bringing the light, which shines away the darkness and the fear. What would our schools, our churches, our governments and our businesses look like if we flip the switch and turn on the light?

As employees it is often easy to avoid taking responsibility by saying "it's not my job" or "I just did what they told me to do" and other pretty lame statements like that. Often what's really going on is that employees are choosing to be powerless instead of powerful or empowered.

Have you heard the story about Bobby, a fourth-string quarterback for a small college who was also the part-time punter? He was a senior, but had never played in even one game. It was one of the last games of the year and during the second quarter, the first-string quarterback got hurt and was taken out of the game. In the third quarter, the second-string quarterback also went down with an injury.

Bobby's team was up 6-3 and it was nearing the end of the game, when, as luck would have it, the third-string quarterback also got hurt and had to come out of the game, which left the coach with no choice but to put Bobby in.

As the offense prepared to take the field at their own 15 yard line, the coach gave Bobby his instructions. "On the first play I want you to take the ball and run to the right. On the second play I want you to run to the left. On the third play I want you to run right up the middle. And on the fourth play I want you to back up and punt the ball."

Bobby ran on to the field with his instructions. On the first play he ran to the right and gained 17 yards. On the second play he ran to the left and broke enough tackles to gain 26 yards. On the third play he ran right up the middle and to the crowd's amazement he broke free, stopped by one guy who tackled him on the 6-inch line. The crowd went crazy. On the fourth play Bobby backed up and punted the ball into the parking lot. The crowd was silent.

The coach came storming on to the field and grabbed Bobby by the shoulder pads and yelled "Bobby! What were you thinking when you punted that ball?????"

Bobby replied, "I was thinking that I must have about the dumbest coach in all of football."

Funny story, but how often does something like this happen in our businesses? "I'm just doing what I was told" is a statement we use when we make the choice to be powerless.

Perhaps the problem is not so much with empowering people as it is having the empowered people own the empowerment. How accountable are we willing to be for the results we get in our own lives?

It used to seem that people only changed to avoid pain. They would finally change something when the pain of changing became less than the pain of staying the same. People prefer the comfortable. But the universe is shifting around us, and it's becoming more and more uncomfortable for people to stay the same. People are choosing uncomfortable familiarity over the unknown which almost always provides a situation that is more comfortable than the previous state, but involves doing something differently.

Maybe that's the rub: doing something DIFFERENTLY means you have to look at the way you've been doing it and make alterations. We don't even have to think about anything to do things the way we've always done them, from work processes to the way we talk to our kids. We just do it that way because it's the way we've always done it. To have to look at that and 1) admit it's not working anymore and 2) do something different in the process, may be too much to expect of ourselves and each other.

What really happens is that it's not the processes and reactions that are difficult to change – it's deeper than that. It comes down to realizing that maybe we aren't the best judge of our own behavior when it comes to relationships in our lives. Sometimes it takes something outside ourselves to remind us of what's really important in the big picture.

A friend was recently on a plane that blew a tire on takeoff. The explosion was felt by everyone in the cabin, and the tension mounted when the pilot told the passengers that they needed to circle the airport for an hour to burn off fuel in the event they needed to make a crash landing. For the next hour this friend and her fellow passengers circled the airport at 3,000 feet where they had internet access to reach out to their friends and families, letting them know that in the worst case, this might be the last communication they would have.

After an hour the plane landed rather uneventfully, but in the full presence of emergency vehicles, sirens and flashing lights. While she was immensely grateful to have landed safely, this friend is also grateful, in hindsight, for that one-hour ordeal where she was able to rethink her priorities. She learned that all her planning and dreaming about what she was going to do with her life could have ended in an instant. It changed her perspective about her purpose.

We all know stories like this one where situations or circumstances outside ourselves caused us to rethink the way we are living our lives. But does it always have to take a tragedy to remind us that we can shift our focus, let down our guard, and gain a deeper meaning for our lives?

This was a question that came up in a recent MasterMind conversation. We were talking about those moments when everything is clicking and we're on a high and all is well with the world. We talked about noticing how we're feeling in those moments and then tracing back to the thought that immediately preceded the feeling. It is possible, we all know, to recreate that experience (or produce one equally as rewarding) yet we still seem to find ourselves in the space of inconsistency.

So it's true that knowing doesn't necessarily equate to doing, which doesn't always produce desired results.

However, as we talked more about this phenomenon, we realized that perhaps the results we are in the process of producing are really at play at a higher level simply because we are aware of the process. In essence, instead of letting our lives run us, we are aware of the fact that we can have a say in the results.

We reminisced about times in our lives when we were on autopilot, or what author and speaker Seth Godin calls "sheepwalking," which he defines as doing things that others tell us to do simply because they said to, which allows us to avoid thinking, coupled with being somewhat brain-dead, especially at work.

Before we knew any better, we would find ourselves muddling through our lives, frustrated and, more often than not, carrying a heavy dose of victim mentality, mindlessly giving up all control of our own outcomes to some unknown and unnamed "them," all the time perpetuating the same results. The best we could come up with for a payoff in those cases was that we could at least be right about our belief that "we" were right and "they" were wrong, and could also prove it by bringing it up to anyone who would listen and agree.

At least now when we notice the results being less than what we want, we know there is another way. It's almost as if there are two of us: the one who is having the experience and the one who is watching the one having the experience. The one who's watching has a much broader view and can much more easily point out alternative ways of thinking and being.

It's actually being in the feeling space - FEELING the feelings and not pushing them away, no matter how "bad" they may be - that allows the feeling to dissipate. What we resist persists and, although we know that in our conscious minds, it's not until it penetrates the old familiar "gotta be right," or what might be called the "yeah, but" space that it has a chance to turn into a new action. New actions produce new results.

1 Peter Koestenbaum and Peter Block, *Freedom and Accountability at Work: Applying Philosophic Insight to the Real World,* (San Francisco: Jossey-Bass/Pfeiffer, 2001), p. 26.
2 Ibid, p. 30.

TOOLS for OWNING RESPONSIBILITY

Conversational Tools:

In response to a statement like: "I have too much to do. I can't get it done."
OK. What is it that takes up the majority of your time? What is bogging you down most? How does that impact your work?

In response to a complaint:
I hear you. There are I things I don't like about what I have to do, too. If you knew that you could spend 80% of your job doing things you enjoyed, would you be willing to devote 20% to tasks and necessities you know have to get done even if you don't love doing them?

In response to a suggestion:
Great idea. Are you willing to take that on? I'm looking for a champion. Is that you?

In response to a compliment:
Thank you for having the courage to say that and the responsibility to notice the positive. It's so easy to see the negative first, so I really appreciate your telling me that.

Experiential Tools

The results these tools produce will be best measured by recording observations in a small notebook or journal. Choose one of the following "assignments" each week and share observations in weekly team meetings or with a MasterMind group.

Drill Down. Drill Down is a simple technique for breaking complex problems down into progressively smaller parts.

To use the technique, start by writing the problem down on the left-hand side of a large sheet of paper. Next, write down the points that make up the next level of detail on the problem a little to the right of this. These may be factors contributing to the problem, information relating to it, or questions raised by it. This process of breaking the problem down into its component part is called "drilling down[1]."

For each of these points, repeat the process. Keep on drilling down into points until you fully understand the factors contributing to the problem. If you cannot break them down using the knowledge you have, then carry out whatever research is necessary to understand the point.

Journaling. Unless you know better, there is no way you can apply new knowledge to a problem or challenge. But if you know better and choose not to do better, that's the same as not knowing at all. As you learn new information and try new ideas, it will serve you well to record those thoughts and ideas in a notebook or journal. As you make a habit of recording your observations, you will be able to track your victories as well as your learning opportunities much more easily.

MasterMinding. Get together with a group of like-minded and like-hearted people to share thoughts, dreams, ideas and support in a spirit of true dialogue (suspending previous assumptions for the purpose of learning from each other). Start by reading a book like *Think and Grow Rich,* where the term MasterMind originates.

When people come together in a spirit of harmony for a definite purpose, the best of all of them is present to support each other for the achievement of whatever they truly desire and are willing to take action toward.

Create an Issue Log. If you make mistakes, which you will if you are human, instead of hiding them to avoid the fear of reprimand, log them. Set the standard for your team or your family, that the reprimand will come if the mistakes are ***NOT*** logged, not if they are.

Here is a format you can follow when logging mistakes:

1) What happened? Describe the situation in as much detail as you can.
2) What was the impact?
3) Who was affected?
4) What future success will we experience from the learning?
5) What will happen if we don't address this situation?

Having high standards does not mean choosing the easy over the difficult. Recalling the Energy section in this book, we learned about the distinction between Pink and Blue. If Pink personalities are more emotional and relational and Blue personalities are more logical and transactional, you might see how they come at mistakes from two different perspectives.

Regardless of which perspective you naturally have, ask yourself if you believe in your team's desired outcome. Do you believe in your shared why? If so, understand that the standards for logging mistakes will help to achieve those outcomes much more quickly. Even if Blues don't want to hear the mistakes, and Pinks don't want to bring them up, without both working together, there is no chance for resolution.

How your team manages the harmony between the Pink and the Blue will be an indication of how successful you will be as teams of families, workplaces, and communities.

Set Micro Goals. Annual, five-year and 10-year goals can help you expand on a personal and professional mission, because you know you are working toward a measurable goal. However, long-term goals are useless unless you have a plan in place to achieve them. Learn to lead yourself by setting micro goals.

While checking random tasks off a to-do list provides some level of satisfaction, micro goals are single actions that, when accomplished, serve as building blocks to a much larger goal.

Hot Air Balloon. Every now and then, especially when you are feeling a bit frustrated in a certain situation, imagine yourself in a hot air balloon tethered 50 feet above the ground. From this perspective, look at the situation which is causing you the anxiety. Do you see another option for the person who looks like you in this situation? Sometimes a mere change of perspective can provide new possibilities you can't see from inside the situation.

Did Well, Do Better. Whenever you accomplish a task or give a speech or presentation, take out a piece of paper and draw a vertical line down the middle. On one side write "Did Well" and on the other side "Do Better Next Time." As you are evaluating your own performance, be honest, but don't be too harsh. Make a note and adjust next time, and you will be on the path to mastery.

DWYSYWD. This is an acronym for Do What You Say You Will Do. Get good at what don Miguel Ruiz calls being impeccable with your word (from *The Four Agreements*). The word impeccable literally means "without sin." And, to drill deeper, sin is "anything you do which goes against yourself." As you practice this skill, you will get better at it, until eventually you will never consider saying anything with which you don't intend to follow through.

Take It From Nike. As the athletic company's brand says, Just Do It. If you don't like your job, instead of complaining about it, find a new one. If you are unhappy with your weight, eat less and exercise more. The key to anything you choose to Just Do is that you make the decision to Just Do It. There is no one to blame (not even yourself), just get on with it.

Don't be like the hound dog lying on the floor of an old general store, moaning and whining. When the owner was asked why his dog was crying, he replied "Oh, there is a nail sticking up from the floorboard and he's lying on top of it. When the pain is great enough, he'll roll off."

What nail are you lying on?

Reward the Discipline. Instead of beating yourself up about goals you don't meet, instead take care of those parts of any transition you can control and give up attachment to the specifics. For example, when you reward the discipline it takes to contact prospective leads for your business, you have no control over whether they decide to hire you or not. However, you do have 100% control over the contacts you make.

Reward the discipline as it relates to the calls, or what you eat, or number of steps you walk. If you are committed (willing to do whatever it takes even when the emotion you said it in wears off) to the discipline, the results will take care of themselves.

My business partner and good friend Don Cote recently told me a story his wise father told him about a boy who lived on a farm. The boy's father wanted to teach him an important life lesson, so when a baby calf was born, the father asked the boy to lift the calf. He was able to do that. Every day the boy was instructed to lift the calf, and every day he was able to do it. Over time, as the calf grew, so did the boy's strength. He eventually was able to lift a cow, not just a calf.

Never doubt the power of discipline and persistence.

Go the Extra Mile. Make it a habit to give more and better service than your customers/associates expect. The opposite of this idea is expecting something for nothing, or anything for less than its value. When you come from a mindset of contribution, sooner or later you will be rewarded for your wisdom, your attitude, and your outlook, and will receive compensation far greater than the actual value of the service you provide.

So said Napoleon Hill in one of his *Mental Dynamite* booklets called *Going the Extra Mile.*

Don't be the person who says "I'm not paid to do that," or "That's not my job." That attitude becomes a mindset, and will prohibit advancement opportunities, to say nothing of negatively impacting the relationships with co-workers and family members.

Quit Trying Harder. Doing the same thing over and over and expecting different results is what Einstein called insanity. Trying harder often produces, at best, incremental gains, resulting in frustration, resignation, and burnout. If you want to experience a desired result, quit trying harder. More effort isn't the answer. You must do something new.

Give yourself permission to dream. To risk. Be willing to sacrifice your old beliefs and reasonable thought patterns. As Price Pritchett says in *You*^{2}, "If you must doubt something, doubt your limits^2."

Commit to shifting gears when you are stuck in a rut and try something different, even if it feels crazy or a bit risky. What do you have to lose except your old results?

Take a Stand. Instead of continuing to fight against what you don't want, determine not what you are willing to die for, but what you are must live for. In *Fierce Conversations* author Susan Scott reminds us "It is not enough to be willing to speak. The time has come for you to speak. Be willing to face mutiny everywhere but in yourself. Your time of holding back, of guarding your private thoughts, is over. Your function in life is to make a declarative statement. Sit beside someone you care for and begin[3]."

1 http://www.free-management-ebooks.com/news/drill-down-technique/
2 Price Pritchett, *You2: A High-Velocity Formula for Multiplying Personal Effectiveness in Quantum Leaps* (Pritchett, LP, no date), p. 16.
3 Susan Scott, *Fierce Conversations: Achieving Success at Work & in Life, One Conversation at a Time* (New York: Berkley Books, 2002), pp. 246-47.

Having the information
and knowing what to do
is only part
of the formula:
**you must
do something**
with what you know.

CONCLUSION

Connecting with your personal POWER is an opportunity to move the results in your life from what you only wish could happen to what you can't help but experience. Having the information and knowing what to do is only part of the formula: you must do something with what you know.

As long as fear keeps you from action and wishful thinking prevents you from riskful thinking and doing, you will never have the possibility of living from and into the thought system needed to transform from who you've been being to who you are becoming.

Get clear on the vision you want for yourself and your life and utilize it to set the foundation for your new outlook. Know that when you are committed, possibility is greater than the probability of staying the same.

You will only be
truly inspired
to transform
if you are
READY
to get beyond fear
to love.

Once you have a clear vision and are ready to take new action, knowledge becomes knowing; blame becomes benevolence; scarcity becomes abundance; and fear becomes love.

Do not settle! Unless you are diligent in the new, the old will creep back in. If you ***hold*** new beliefs but don't ***live*** them, you will suffer the consequences.

You will never truly experience the new without giving up the previous. That is the distinction between change and transformation.

Good news: if anything here has resonated with you, the seeds have already been planted. The fact that you picked up the book at all proves that you are at least ***READY*** for a new challenge.

And the fact that you've read this far in the book, proves that you are ***ABLE*** to take this on. The only thing that's missing, then, is the ***WILLINGNESS***. You need to bring that. You need to decide – to cut off the other options – and move forward.

Remember, you attract not what you want, but who you really are. So if you allow your fear of change to creep back in, you will realize that you weren't as ready as you might have thought you were when you picked up this book.

The truth will come out – you will only be truly inspired to transform if you are READY to get beyond fear to love.

Authenticity can't be supported when there is no heart and soul and spirit. And that's a problem with traditional corporate structures.

If you really think about it, the word "corporate" has as its root "corpus," which refers to the body, the bones, the structure. That corporate structure doesn't include heart, soul or spirit. Is there a possibility to love where you are even if it's not perfect?

Are your employees open to learning and growth? Have you attracted those people by who you are being as leaders inside those corporate structures?

Even if this isn't your life purpose, can you find something inside your structure that allows you to be you? If you are ***WILLING*** to do the worst job from a good place, that shows who you are so you can advance to other things. The energy of ***DOING*** comes from ***BEING***.

MYTH: You need to do something specific to get your desired result, and if you don't discover what that is and do it, you can't get the result. **REALITY**: Your life is not like baking a cake. There are many ways to get a cake, and only one of them includes baking it yourself. Following a recipe from scratch, or making it from a box, asking a friend to share a piece cake at a bakery, or manifesting someone bringing cake to your door: all are ways to get the desired result. It's not always the long process you do to get what you want. True desire is different. It's about deciding and allowing. It's not about judging the process.

The process is like planting seeds. Understanding you need to deposit before you withdraw. Cultivate because you don't know for sure what's going to grow. You know cake. You know planting a carrot seed means that in 47 days you have a carrot. You don't know about these intangibles. Many people stop visualizing and end up leaving trails of potential behind them. What if you gave up attachment to the how and got really serious about the what and the why? Who knows what will come from possibilities when you are present and intentional and unattached?

Who you ARE is enough. If you are interested but not yet intentional, you will know. When you are truly committed, you will know that, too.

Your belief is based on the past. You can only believe something you know about. When that belief drags you down because its energy is negative, be mindful not to drag it into your future.

The changes you will notice in your leadership and relationships will occur to you differently than before, and wherever you are on your journey is exactly where you are supposed to be. This is no ***should*** in this manual for your life.

Your perceived lack, uncertainty, discomfort, disrespect, all have come from past experience. Wisdom is your ability to leave behind whatever will no longer serve you and step into a whole new experience without fear dragging you down.

It is only your uncertainty that will cause you to fear the choices you have in front of you.

Take your tools and study them. Ponder your impact. Let it go – move forward lightly and travel lightly.

Notice what you notice and take responsibility.

Don't be surprised when you get what you ask for. And don't be surprised if it looks different than you intended.

The time is NOW. The world needs you – completely and authentically. Step into your POWER and model the way. The toolbox is here for you.

BOOKS AND RESOURCES mentioned in *P.O.W.E.R. Tools @ Work* (In the order presented)

Delivering Happiness by Tony Hsieh

John Maxwell, author of several leadership books

Drive: The Surprising Truth About What Motivates Us by Daniel Pink

Good to Great by Jim Collins

Think and Grow Rich by Napoleon Hill

Flow: The Psychology of Optimal Experience by Mihaly Csikszentmihalyi

Is Your Genius At Work? by Dick Richards

Principles by Ray Dalio

What Got You Here Won't Get You There by Marshall Goldsmith

Outwitting the Devil by Napoleon Hill

Wisdom @ Work: The Making of a Modern Elder by Chip Conley

The Desire Map by Danielle LaPorte

Pitch Like a Girl by Ronna Lichtenberg

The Science of Getting Rich by Wallace D. Wattles

QBQ: The Question Behind the Question by John G. Miller

The Answer to How is Yes by Peter Block

Freedom and Accountability at Work by Peter Block and Peter Koestenbaum

The Art of Possibility by Ben and Roz Zander

The 100/0 Principle by Al Ritter

A New Earth by Eckhart Tolle

The Four Agreements by don Miguel Ruiz

Going the Extra Mile by Napoleon Hill

You^2 by Price Pritchett

Fierce Conversations by Susan Scott

ACKNOWLEDGMENTS

Jodee thanks:

Brenda, for taking the bull (me) by the horns (which, if you think about it, is kind of a stupid and dangerous thing to do) and giving me the firepower to get this done. Your design eye makes everything beautiful.

Kelly Meyer, for always being willing to drop whatever you're doing to walk me through a process or talk me off the cliff. You are a magical soul sister and I am blessed to be on this journey with you.

Don Cote, my amazing soul brother. We are up to big things, and I'm so grateful for your mentorship, leadership, partnership, and mostly friendship. I'm blessed and grateful to share in, witness, and celebrate the success of LifeWorks University.

Napoleon Hill for *Think and Grow Rich* and my POWER4 MasterMinders: **Ed**, **Theresa, David**, and **Dody**. Wednesdays are better because of each of you.

Saturday MasterMinders: **Lauri**, **Kelly**, **Jeff**, **Allen**, **Ryan**, and **Carrie**. I so appreciate each of you for being bold and brave and a bit crazy to get up on Saturday mornings for the past 10+ years to learn and grow with me. I so appreciate your energy and the learning space you provide, and I love who we are becoming, both individually and collectively.

Lauri Winterfeldt, **Amanda Brannan** and **Saree Reveling**: thank you so much for your editing and honest feedback. I'm so grateful for each of you.

The staffs of Caribou on 45th and Caribou at Gateway Hornbachers for allowing us to use your space to create. Thanks for the caffeine and the support!

And, continuing with the tradition, here's the shoutout to Rosanne Bane, who noted in her book Dancing in the Dragon's Den, that the main reason anyone reads the acknowledgements is to see whether they were mentioned. So thank you, ____________________ (insert your name here), for your interest in *P.O.W.E.R. Tools @ Work*. Let's use these tools to enhance our cultures and live the way we were meant to live in all aspects of our lives.

Brenda thanks:

First and foremost **Jodee** for inviting me to share in my first MasterMind group more than a decade ago. The concepts I have been able to implement in my life and the relationships I have developed as a result of these incredible groups have truly changed the trajectory of my life.

Tom Levos for being my rock and biggest supporter. Without question there is no one I would want to be on this crazy ride called life with. Thank you for helping me recognize my own POWER.

Hope & Megan for walking with me all these years on this adventure. Your strength, perseverance and loving hearts inspire me each day to be a better person and a stronger woman. It is my hope that you embrace your own POWER and chase the lives of your dreams.

ABOUT JODEE

Jodee Bock is an accidental entrepreneur who started her own business, Bock's Office Transformational Consulting, in response to a series of career moves which highlighted those elements she didn't even realize were missing. She is grateful for her decision to leave Corporate America, because she is committed to helping people stay and thrive in those organizations, supports people in the areas of leadership, communication, and accountability.

She is a native North Dakotan who, despite the cold winters, appreciates the warm hearts of those in her physical space. She is also growing her global reach as Dean of LifeWorks University, an online learning center where students work together in MasterMind groups to support each other in living the lives of their dreams. Find more information about LifeWorks at www.lifeworks.university.

Jodee is the author of several books, including *The 100% Factor*, the *Own Your Story* series, *Say What?*, and a co-author, with Brenda, of *Inviting Dialogue*. She sings with the award-winning City of Lakes barbershop chorus and enjoys her "job" as the head scorekeeper for the NDSU men's and women's basketball teams.

ABOUT BRENDA

Brenda Levos is a wildly creative designer, photographer, artist, mother, wife, friend, and an avid reader and lifelong learner.

She loves having great conversations about how to live an authentic life, inspired and fully living your genius. She is a master of manifestation, and is enjoying the results of that skill in her new lake home in Minnesota and her new career path as Strategic Communications Coordinator at HDR, a global firm that designs solutions to the world's greatest challenges.

She also maintains her own graphic design business where she works on projects like this one, and is dedicated to utilizing her creativity in unexpected ways. She has participated in, and co- facilitated, various MasterMind groups and continues to be inspired by the amazing outcomes she witnesses in these groups as well as with her own family.

Brenda has many varied interests including, but certainly not limited to, painting, baking, printmaking, stained glass, sculpture, travel, and photography.

She and her husband Tom are the parents of two daughters, Hope and Megan, and their fur baby Molly. They split time between their lake cabin in Minnesota and their family farm in rural southeastern North Dakota.

But Wait ... There's More!

P.O.W.E.R. Tools @ Work is not only a book,it is also a day-long learning workshop facilitated by Jodee Bock, Brenda Levos, or other certified facilitators.

In the workshop your teams will have an opportunity to dig deeper into each of the five areas and leave with action items to support your shared vision.

If you are interested in learning more about how *P.O.W.E.R. Tools @ Work* could be used in your organization, about becoming certified to deliver the associated day-long workshop, or keeping updated on our ever-expanding toolbox, please visit our website: www.powertoolsatwork.com/moretools.

We know there are many ways to enhance corporate cultures and are grateful you're interested in using this resource to do just that.

Whatever your title or position, inside or outside corporate cultures, you have the ability to enhance the lives of anyone to whom you come into contact.

Thank you for taking on that challenge! We look forward to working with you to keep people inspired, engaged, and connected.

Thank you

Thank you for your commitment to your own and your organization's success. When you are willing to do whatever it takes to achieve a result (without violating the rights of others), the universe will conspire on your behalf.

So, now it's time to take some action. Use these tools. Produce some results so you can adjust as you go. Remember, this is a process.

And when you have some results you're excited about, please let us know! We'd love to hear about and share your successes.

Go to the website
www.powertoolsatwork.com/successes
and upload away!